D1147247

World War I Army Ancestry

NORMAN HOLDING

Published by the
Federation of Family History Societies (Publications) Ltd.,
The Benson Room, Birmingham and Midland Institute,
Margaret Street, Birmingham B3 3BS, England.

First edition 1982
Second edition 1991
Third edition 1997

ISBN 1 86006 056 2

Printed and bound by the Alden Group, Oxford

CONTENTS

ACKNOWLEDGEMENTS

The author would like to express his thanks to Major (Retd) C.W.P. Coan of the Royal Corps of Transport Museum and to Col. (Retd) A.V. Tennuci of the Royal Army Medical Corps Museum who have provided help from, and access to, their records; to the staff of the Imperial War Museum for their willing cooperation; to the Keeper of Records, Public Record Office, for granting permission to reproduce the extract from the War Diary; to the staff of the Luton Central Library who have made numerous journeys to the stack to locate dusty volumes and for obtaining a continuous supply of obscure books via the inter-library loan service; to Col. I.S. Swinnerton for details of some of the sources and his helpful suggestions; to J.M.A. Tamplin for his help with medal records and his encouraging letters; to Brian Craddock for use of his letter and G.W. Boswell who proved that old soldiers can be traced.

Lastly to my friends and colleagues who have provided hints, tips and an ear during the search; to Margaret Adams for the typing of the draft from my illegible handwriting for the first edition, to Pauline Litton for her proof reading second time around and to my wife who refrained from tidying my piles of notes into the waste bin.

The extract from A.F. Becke's book *Order of Battle of Divisions* published by H.M.S.O. which forms Figures 6 and 7 is reproduced by permission of the Controller of H.M. Stationery Office.

The facsimile page from WO95/411-PRO Kew reproduced in Figure 8 is a Crown copyright record in the Public Record Office and appears by permission of the Controller of H.M. Stationery Office.

FAMILY RECORDS CENTRE/ST CATHERINE'S HOUSE

Readers should note that St Catherine's House is now closed. All records formerly held there, including the indexes to Births, Marriages and Deaths in England and Wales from 1837, are now in the Office for National Statistics section of the Family Records Centre at 1 Myddelton Street, Islington, London EC1R 1UW.

FOREWORD

Having spent over a year tracing the activities of my late father during his period of War service in France 1916-19, I have now collected a considerable amount of information which I feel would be of interest to those wishing to carry out similar research. The result is this booklet which will act as a guide to those who, like myself, started from scratch with almost no knowledge of the history, military organisation or records of World War I.

As my father served in a Motor Ambulance Convoy manned by both the Army Service Corps and the Royal Army Medical Corps, my notes do have a bias in that direction. Similarly, the only theatre of operations referred to is France, but most of the sources deal with men and units who served in the many other campaigns.

My lack of knowledge of things military causes me some concern, as I am sure I have made some glaring mistakes for which I apologise. I can only hope that those for whom this book is intended are not misled and by the time they know enough to point out my errors, they themselves will be experts on their own ancestors' activities. Should they uncover other sources on the way, I would be delighted to hear of them so that any later editions can be more informative.

N. Holding
June 1982

FOREWORD TO 1991 EDITION

In the nine years since this book first appeared, many books on various aspects of the War have appeared, but to my knowledge this still remains the only one, apart from my own companion volumes, which acts as a guide to those trying to trace the service of their ancestors. This is a pity. With so much interest, as shown by the sales and the need to update, I would have welcomed some competition. I have added a few of the new books to the bibliography and also mentioned those which are now being reprinted. Apart from minor corrections the main additions are references to the few additional items available at the Public Record Office, Kew. The main records, still retained by the Ministry of Defence, will not be available for another six years. After the 1992 release of the 1891 Census, roll on 1996!

N. Holding
January 1991

FOREWORD TO 1997 EDITION

The need to reprint means that a few small errors can be corrected and a paragraph or two can be added to report the release of the first batch of Soldiers' Papers from the War period in 1996. I must again express my thanks to Iain Swinnerton for pointing out so many of the errors.

N. Holding
May 1997

1

INTRODUCTION

Anyone who served in the First World War 1914–18, or, as it was known at one time, the Great War must be at least 90 and it would be a more reasonable assumption that they would be nearer a hundred. Anyone under 90 would have very little memory of life in those times. This means that already one of the most costly wars in history, at least in terms of soldiers' lives, is passing rapidly into the realms of Family History and Genealogy. For most people the question, 'What did grandfather or father do in the War?' is already being asked too late. The ancestors have died leaving behind a few photos, a medal or two and hopefully a collection of reminiscences passed on to their children.

With over 5 million men serving in the forces from the British Isles alone and many women, both at home and overseas, in hospital work, there can be few people who did not have at least one close ancestor involved in the War (Note 1).

For those who wish to record a history of their ancestors' war experiences it is almost too late. The most vital of the records, the 'Parish Registers' of army research, have already been destroyed and no 'Bishops Transcripts' or copies exist. This booklet sets out to provide the Family History researchers with a list of sources available to them so that they may reconstruct the career of a soldier. Although it provides a few clues, it does not attempt to lay down research methods as these must depend to a large extent on the individual case. Moreover, the contents are mainly concerned with Army NCOs and private soldiers. Officers, being somewhat easier to deal with, are not considered except in passing. A large part is taken up with references to sources and books, although the latter is far from being a complete list. Some of the references and notes are not mentioned in the text so the reader is advised to read them all.

2

THE RECORDS

During a soldier's career his name must have been written down many times. Firstly when he signed on, then on his first posting to a training unit. Later his name would be put on a leave list, a transfer list upon going to another unit or being posted overseas. If he was promoted, his name would appear in Company Orders; if he won a medal, the recommendation would be passed back to his Divisional HQ; if he was wounded, the Medical Orderly wrote down the details; if he was killed, he was recorded once more even if his death took place in the mud of no-mans-land and his body was never found. Finally, at the end of the war came the discharge; once more his name was recorded and his service and campaign medals awarded. With so many records, tracing a man over the four years of the war should be easy. Unfortunately, the numbers of men and the quantity of records involved made the task of storage too great; as a result many papers were destroyed before 1939. Those that survived the rigours of the Civil Service and the War Office suffered under Hitler's bombardment and these too are lost. The most significant of the latter were the personnel records of the five million soldiers. This single event means that almost any chance of finding the ancestor's name in a list or other record made during the war has vanished.

A few items remain and these are becoming available for public search. A small batch of about 8% of the Soldiers' Papers are now in the Public Record Office, Kew but most remain in the hands of the Ministry of Defence who will search for a name on payment of a fee. It is no longer necessary to prove kinship.

The ancestor's name can be found in the following sources.

(a) The surviving personnel service records.
(b) The remaining casualty lists.
(c) The Medal Rolls.
(d) The medal list in the London Gazette.
(e) The list of soldiers who died in the First World War.
(f) The Grave List.
(g) The War Diary of the unit in which he served; most unlikely for other ranks.
(h) The Death Certificate in the Family Records Centre, Myddelton Street.

Of these, the first is limited to the 8% in the Public Record Office and the remaining 30% of 'Burnt Docs' still with the MoD. For anyone who survived the war unscathed only the Medal Roll is likely to produce his name. If this lack of information does not discourage you, then the remainder of this booklet will provide sufficient details to build up at least a picture of the ancestor's life in the Army even if at the end of the research much will be based on assumption and deduction.

3

FAMILY RECORDS

As in any genealogical research project, the first task is to gather together all family documents and oral data on the ancestor. These are likely to include photographs, letters, medals and perhaps the occasional official document such as a discharge certificate. Shortly after the war started it was an offence, even for officers, to have cameras or to keep diaries. However, the large numbers of books and collections of personal diaries in the Imperial War Museum Library give hope that many men disobeyed both orders. Both in England and on the Continent many professional photographers made a living taking photographs of single soldiers or of groups, so most men were able to send pictures of themselves in uniform back to their loved ones in England. Although these were endorsed *somewhere in France* they usually carry a date. By careful examination of the photographs, one should be able to determine the Regiment or Corps from the various buttons and badges. Years of service can be estimated from service and good conduct stripes. Postmarks will enable the dates of embarkation to be tied down as far as possible, i.e. between the last letter posted in England and first in France. With luck, and most research depends on luck, you may find a photo taken after the war when censorship was finished. This will give a date and a location other than *somewhere in France.* Letters sent to the soldier are also valuable. They often give the unit of the ancestor in the address. Read all the letters and cards to obtain any clue.

What you are trying to obtain is information on:

Dates (can they be deduced from the contents or postmarks?).

Postings and locations.

Name of Unit (Regiment, Corps – if possible the Battalion or Unit number).

Medals (is he wearing a ribbon or do you have it?).

Army number (may be on the medal or a letter).

Years of service (from dates and service stripes).

Type of work (background to pictures might show a stable or workshop).

Don't forget to look at his companions if it is a group photo, the badges etc. may be clearer in the front row.

The next move is to check the photos with the pictures of badges and other insignia as shown in the various reference books (Refs. 39–44 and 65). Do not be surprised if the badges show a different unit to that given by other sources. It was not uncommon for men to transfer or be transferred to other units. In 1917 for instance, many men were taken out of the Army Service Corps and transferred to front line infantry units. Wounded or elderly men were frequently moved to the Labour Corps for work behind the lines.

At this point, it would be as well to search for the name in the *National Roll of Honour* (Ref. 36) but copies may be difficult to locate. Some libraries have the volumes which cover their own town. If it is known that the ancestor died in action, then a search should be made in the Miscellaneous Section of the Records of Births, Marriages and Deaths in the Family Records Centre (Ref. 6), in *Soldiers Died in the Great War* (Ref. 35) or in the Imperial War Graves Commission Cemetery lists (Ref. 37). If you have not found out the ancestor's regiment and battalion by now, the search of the second item can be time-consuming as the hundred-odd volumes are indexed by regiment. However, the finding of an entry will be most rewarding – a lot of additional information may be given. Remember that the numbers involved are very high and even rare surnames can be found with identical Christian names in different regiments. Make sure you have found the right one. It is safer to search the lot unless you are 100% sure.

The Cemetery list is also worth searching, as it gives next of kin. This time, it is important to know where the ancestor died so that the cemetery can be identified otherwise about another hundred volumes will have to be searched. The Commonwealth War Graves Commission at Maidenhead may be able to help here (Ref. 37).

Family tradition or oral information should not be neglected. The tales passed down may recall a particular town or battle, even the address of a French girlfriend may provide evidence of a period of time spent in a certain village. Tradition may also give the name of a Regiment or type of work – 'He drove lorries full of shells' or 'I spent the war filling in leave permits and never got one for myself' or, again, 'Major Blenkinsop my old CO would never have allowed it'.

Such remarks provide a good clue that can be followed up but do not be fooled by mention of Ypres or the Somme. There were four battles of Ypres and only two of the 50 odd Divisions did **not** fight on the Somme.

There are a number of items which the family may still have. If the ancestor was wounded and discharged he would have been sent a silver badge inscribed *For King and Empire: Services Rendered*. If he died, then besides a telegram and a letter from his CO, the next of kin were sent a 4¼″ diameter brass plaque with his name engraved on it. The design of the plaque was based on the winning entry of a competition held in 1919. It depicts a figure of Britannia and a lion. The plaques were issued in 1919 in cardboard containers within a white envelope bearing the Royal Crest. In a separate cardboard roll each recipient also had an 11″ × 7″ scroll recording that the soldier died *that others might live in freedom* and giving his Rank, Name and Regiment. Also enclosed was a letter from the King. (See *Swinnerton Family History Journal,* No 4, January 1980. See also Note 12.)

For Christmas 1914 all members of the British Expeditionary Force received a card from the king. This was inscribed *May God protect you and bring you home safe.* In 1915 all wounded in hospital received a similar card.

If you still have the ancestor's medals, these will give positive details of his Regiment, Corps, Number and Rank, but not perhaps his unit or battalion. The three most common ones are Pip, Squeak and Wilfred (after three characters in a newspaper cartoon) or, more correctly, 'The 1914 Star' (often called the 'Mons Star'), the 'British War Medal' and the 'Victory Medal'.

The 1914 star was a bronze four-pointed star behind crossed swords, superimposed with a crowned wreath. A central scroll is inscribed '1914'. This was given to officers and men who served with a unit in France or Belgium between 5th August 1914 and midnight on 22nd/23rd November 1914. A bar bearing the words 5 Aug.–22 Nov '14 was added to the ribbon for those who served under the fire of the enemy. When the ribbon only was worn a small Rosette was added to this ribbon to indicate the 'under fire' bar. A 1914–15 Star was also issued which was almost the same in design but the wording on the scroll reads '1914–15'. This was for those who served up to 31st December 1915 but did not have the 1914 Star. However, the service could be in a far wider geographical area.

A Territorial Force Medal in bronze was awarded to all men who volunteered for overseas service before 30th September 1914 and who had already served in the Territorials for four years before 4th August 1914.

The British War Medal is silver and bears an effigy of the King and on the reverse Saint George on horseback. The Victory Medal is bronze and shows a winged figure of Victory. The ribbon of the latter can carry a small bronze oak leaf denoting one or more *Mentions in Despatches.* Both medals were given to those who served overseas for a period between 5th August 1914 and 11th November 1918. The Victory Medal was given only to those who served in a theatre of war.

If you find that the ancestor was awarded a gallantry medal or was mentioned in despatches, check the entry in the *London Gazette.* This was issued daily and included long supplements of medal recipients and those mentioned in despatches. The lists were usually arranged in alphabetical order within Regiments and Corps. If you do not know which one it takes a long time to search. The issues containing the lists can be located in the quarterly indexes. After 1916, individual names of recipients as well as the issue number are given in the indexes.

Look under *State Intelligence – War Office.* Sets of the *London Gazette* can be found in only a few of the larger libraries and some do not have an index. The Guildhall Library has a complete set and the indexes are on open shelves. A similar set is in the Public Record Office, look in Class Z, together with index volumes for the War Years which are on open shelves in the Microfilm Room. When calling for the required bound monthly volume, take care – the index does not give the volume number, only page numbers which run right through a year's issues (12 volumes). The counter staff have a conversion list – page number to month, and hence volume for each year.

4

MEDAL ROLLS AT THE PUBLIC RECORD OFFICE, KEW

The Medal Rolls which were at one time at the Medal Office at Droitwich have now been transferred to the Public Record Office at Kew. There are a number of leaflets which researchers will find of use.

No. 101, Service Medals and Award Rolls, War of 1914–18.

Leaflet No. 101 covers the use of records dealing with Service Medals. These are the British War Medal, Victory Medal, 1914 Star, 1914–1915 Star, Territorial Force War Medal and the Silver War Badge (for soldiers discharged wounded). The records and the indexes to which the leaflet refers are for officers and other ranks in the Army and the Royal Flying Corps and form part of Classes WO329 and WO372.

No. 105, First World War; Indexes to Medal Entitlement.

This covers the DCM, MSM, MM and Mentions in Despatches. It also has information regarding the *London Gazette,* a set of which is also in the Public Record Office in Class ZJ1.

No. 108, Records of Medals.

This is a more general leaflet which covers all medals, for all Services, for all periods. It has a list of PRO Class numbers for medal rolls.

The indexes to Service Medals, as described in leaflet No. 101, are on 25,000 microfiche housed in small filing cabinets on a table in the centre of the Microfilm Reading Room. They have the Class number WO372. You select a viewer and take the numbered dummy fiche from your viewer to the cabinets, locate the required fiche and replace it with the dummy. After viewing the fiche, return it to the correct place, marked by your dummy. Take only one fiche at a time. The fiche collection contains images of about 9 million index cards, usually one per soldier. The arrangement of the cards on the fiche is not straightforward. Each fiche has six rows each of 12 frames. Each frame shows six index cards arranged as follows: at the left-hand side of the frame, three cards one under the other in the order 1, 2, 3 with 1 at the top. On the right-hand side of the frame, three cards one under the other in the order 4, 5, 6. Thus No. 4 is at the top of the frame. Therefore to search in sequence one must move along the top row of frames whilst moving down and up each column of three in turn. The names are in strict alphabetical order of surnames although the usual warning of mis-spelling and misfiling always applies in addition to uncertainties of the position of 'Mac' or 'Mc' and of hyphenated surnames. Within each surname there are several alphabetical sequences, the first for single initials followed by that for one Christian name. Then comes one name plus one initial, followed by two Christian names and lastly three Christian names, e.g. first comes SMITH, A. to SMITH, Z.; followed by SMITH, Abel to SMITH, Zack; then SMITH, Adam A. to SMITH, Zack Z.; and SMITH, Jack, A.D. to SMITH, Zack Z.Z. This means that, with common surnames, three or more sequences must be searched to ensure that the correct card is found. As it is well known that some people did not always use their full set of given names, all sequences should be searched anyway. Should two or more soldiers have the same names, they are listed in Regimental Order of Preference.

The index cards show name, Regiment, rank and service number. This is usually only the Regiment or Corps and does not give details of the battalion, battery or other unit. Against each listed medal a code number leads the researcher to the ledger containing the record of issue of the medal. Using the finding aid (WO329/1) on a table top in the Microfilm Reading Room, the code number can be converted to the PRO reference number in Class WO329. Photocopies of the Record Cards can be obtained. A further code gives the Operational Theatres of War for which the medal was awarded. A list of these codes is given in *Army Service Records in the First World War* by S. Fowler, W. Spencer and S. Tamblin, published by the Public Record Office, Kew. The ledgers rarely give any more details than those given on the index cards. The dates listed on the cards for the 1914 Star and the 1914–1915 Star show when the recipient entered the Operational Theatres of War to qualify for the medal. The date given in the ledger for the Silver War Badge is the date the recipient joined the army, which is not necessarily the same date as that on which he joined the unit from which he was discharged. Some cards and/or ledgers also give the date of discharge or death.

5

SERVICE RECORDS

In common with soldiers from 1760 onwards, those who served in the First World War had a personnel file recording their complete Army service. As with the pre-1914 records, many WWI files have been lost. During the Second World War, 60% of the files were destroyed through enemy action. The remaining files were badly damaged by fire and water and are stored at the Ministry of Defence at Hayes. The 33,000 boxes take up about 3.2km of shelving. For obvious reasons they are called the 'Burnt Docs'. They are not yet available for public viewing but are being filmed and as each batch is completed the films will appear in Class WO363. The first batch, A–E, will be completed by 1998 and the rest will follow in reverse order, i.e. Z–F. The task is not expected to be completed until 2002. The original records will never be released because of their fragile condition. For a non-returnable fee of £20 (as at January 1997), the MoD will search these remaining records and provide either a typed summary or photocopies if the particular record can be found. These service records are available to any member of the public. Apply for details to: Ministry of Defence, CS(RM) 2, Bourne Avenue, Hayes, Middlesex UB3 1RF.

To try to provide replacements for the destroyed documents, a duplicate partial set was made up with records stored at the Ministry of Pensions. These became known as the 'Unburnt Docs'. These have now been transferred to the Public Record Office. They represent about 10% of those who served and these have now been filmed. The 4000 films are in alphabetical order and are in Class WO364. Unlike the Medal Roll index cards, the names are arranged in orthodox alphabetical order of surname and Christian name(s) but mis-spellings and incorrect sequencing do occur. A copy of the Class List is available on top of the film storage cabinets. **NOTE** A second sequence of names on three or four film rolls appears at the end of the Class List. Don't forget to check both!

The files in Class WO364 contain records of men and women who fall into a number of classes. It is unlikely that those who died during the war without having dependants to whom a pension could be paid are included nor are those who were discharged at the end of the war without a pension. Most of the records concern men who were pre-war soldiers who had been discharged on completion of service before 1920 or records of men who were discharged on medical grounds before 1920 and who had joined before or after 1914 and could have served either with or without overseas service. The records of some pre-war soldiers who rejoined in 1914 and were then discharged during the war are known to have been filed in the last batch (1883–1913) of Soldiers' Papers in WO97/...

A personal inspection for names from the author's own family revealed an increase of about 25% in the number known to have served, many of whom were, in fact, discharged through ill health, some after only a few weeks in the Army. The medical reports on these men revealed medical conditions so obvious that one wonders how they were accepted in the first place.

In preparation for the release of the film of Unburnt Docs in November 1996, Lesley Wynne-Davis and her team from the Friends of the Public Record Office conducted a survey of the documents held at Hayes. A search for the records of soldiers listed in the Medal Rolls in both the Unburnt Docs and the Burnt Docs revealed papers for between 20% and 33% of those in the Medal Rolls. The rest must be considered to have been destroyed in the bombing. In each case, papers for a few additional soldiers, not mentioned in the Medal Rolls, can be found among the Unburnt Docs (i.e. WO364). The lost documents appeared to be distributed among all Regiments and Corps and no one group appears to have suffered from being nearest to the bomb's impact. Although the records are now in strict alphabetical order, they were known at one time to have been arranged in order of Regiments. This can be confirmed by a few filing mistakes. On the whole, however, little is known of the history of the documents and there is much uncertainty about the filing system. Further details of these 1914–18 Soldiers' Papers can be found in the PRO book on the subject. (Ref. 17.)

Official lists of wounded were issued at frequent intervals by the Deputy Adjutant General's Office. Some of these lists were published in part in *The Times,* and extracts in 'local' newspapers. From August 1917 the list appeared weekly and a set has been preserved in the Newspaper Library, Colindale, London. It is not indexed and a search for one man means a search of the whole volume, day after day for every type of casualty. There is no known example of the pre-August 1917 daily lists.

6

ARMY ORGANISATION

You should now be in the position of knowing if the ancestor was in a Corps or a Regiment and as the method of further search depends to a certain extent on which type of unit, you should understand the main differences.

Regiments

These are the traditional fighting units with names such as the King's Own Yorkshire Light Infantry or the Durham Light Infantry. A list is provided in Appendix I. A Regiment usually had two battalions during peace time; each of approximately 1,000 men plus, in many cases, one or more Territorial Battalions. These Territorials were part time soldiers who trained with the Regiment in their spare time for a retainer. The 1st Battalion was frequently stationed overseas to help keep the flag flying over the Empire while the 2nd Battalion remained at home to train new recruits. Each Regiment had a depot or HQ in a town usually associated with it, such as the county town.

With the outbreak of war, the number of recruits increased many fold and extra battalions were formed. At the same time the Territorials were called to full time service. A Regiment could often have more than 10 Battalions and these, although they bore the Regiment's name and wore its insignia, were allocated throughout the army as separate independent units. The 1st and 2nd might serve in France while the 5th was in Egypt. It is thus important to know with which Battalion the ancestor served. The Battalions were identified by a number which can take several forms.

1st   Mummersets (which means 1st Battalion Mummerset Regiment. Most Regiments had two regular battalions; 1st and 2nd. The 3rd, and sometimes the 4th, were for reservists).

5th   Mummersets (which means 5th Battalion Mummerset Regiment, which was usually the Territorial Battalion.)

1/5th Mummersets (which means the First Line Battalion of the 5th Territorial Battalion of the Mummerset Regiment. It was renamed from the 5th Battalion a few days after the start of the War.)

2/5th Mummersets (which means the 2nd Line Battalion of the 5th Territorial Battalion. It was formed to take on new recruits and those men who did not volunteer for overseas service at the outbreak of war.)

10th Mummersets (one of the many new Regiments formed during the War.)

A Regiment thus consisted of a number of battalions each of around 1,000 men. Troops in a Regiment were, in nearly all cases, fighting soldiers, mostly infantry although there were a number of cavalry Regiments. Included in the nominal number of 1,000 were a number of non-fighting personnel who nevertheless were still members of the battalion. They could include

Stretcher bearers — up to 32 when going into battle.

Cooks.

Bandsmen — can act as additional stretcher bearers.

Batmen — Officers' servants.

Transport Drivers. Each battalion had to provide men for its collection of hand carts and horse drawn wagons which carried kit, tents and other equipment.

This reduced the fighting strength to about 800 men. Some Battalions, usually of low medical grade men, were stationed for general duties in depots and HQs. Others had the suffix '(Labour)' or '(Pioneer)'and were used for behind-the-line labouring jobs.

Corps

The word 'corps' is used with three different meanings which can be very confusing for the non-military minded ancestor researcher. In this current context, the word means a large unit of specialised troops. Examples would be the Medical Corps, Army Service Corps and the Royal Regiment of Artillery (the latter is not strictly a Corps but presents the same problems to the researcher as the Regiment was divided into so many artillery Brigades).

The Corps were far larger than the Regiments — the ASC had over 300,000 men — and they were not associated with a town or county. At the Corps HQ men would be trained in the skills appropriate to the Corps and then assembled into self-contained units to carry out a particular function. Because of the need for skilled men the pay was several times that of the infantry soldier. On the other hand, the medical standards of the individuals were frequently lower.

Each Corps would have many types of unit for carrying out the multitude of tasks necessary to keep an army in fighting condition. The ASC had over 10 types of unit involved with transport alone. A list of some of the more common Corps unit types is given in Appendix III. The size of the units depended on their function and was laid down in their War Establishment (page 24, q.v.) but in general was far smaller than that of an Infantry Battalion. In 1915, for example, an ASC Field Ambulance Workshop, an ASC unit, consisted of only 20 men.

Some units could be even smaller. As an added complication some men were 'attached' to a unit of another Corps but had no unit number of their own. Thus the establishment of a Field Ambulance — a RAMC unit of some 200 men — included 45 ASC personnel. This meant that the number of units in a Corps was far higher than the number of Battalions in a Regiment. Moreover, it was not usual to give the name or number of the unit in the various sources mentioned so far. This means that the family historian has a problem.

With Regiments, the task is to identify, with the aid of Regimental Histories, the ancestor's battalion out of, perhaps, 10 such units. This can usually be done fairly easily from books that are available in the local library. With Corps, the number of units could run to over a thousand, involving perhaps 100 different types, and as the histories of Corps units are very specialised, books are hard to come by nor do they often mention specific units by name or number.

When dealing with men who served with one of the Corps and not knowing the unit number, the search can be very long indeed. Even when a unit has been identified there is only a slim chance of proving that the correct one has been found.

Armies, Corps and Divisions

The general organisation of our armies in France must also be mentioned in order that an overall picture can be formed as, without this, the searcher will not be able to locate those records which still remain. (Figs. 4—7.)

Directly under the command of the GHQ were the 5 Armies. These Armies were formed at different times and the numbers given to each also changed. The GHQ also had control of a number of 'Lines of Communication Troops' who were often Corps units which provided the basic services for the British Armies, depots, transport, base hospitals etc. (see examples in Appendix III). At various times some of these units would be allocated by GHQ to one of the Armies on a temporary basis and they would thus report to that Army's HQ instead of GHQ.

Each Army also had its 'Army Troops' who likewise were mostly Corps units to provide basic services for that Army. They did, however, include one or more Battalions of infantry, usually made up of low medical grade men for general duties around the HQ. Once again the General in command of the Army could allocate some of his Army Troops to report directly to the next echelon down. This was the Army Corps (see Ref. 66) — not to be confused with the Corps previously mentioned. The word 'army' is usually omitted thus adding to the confusion. Army Corps were usually written in the form XXI Corps. Each Army had three or four Army Corps of fighting men or roughly three or four times 80,000 men, say 250,000—300,000 per Army.

Army Corps were subdivided into four to six Divisions plus the usual service troops called Army Corps Troops although, again, the word 'Army' is usually omitted. Divisions were the main fighting unit. They tended to be kept together without change throughout the war. On the other hand, the allocation of Divisions to Army Corps and Army Corps to Armies was changed very frequently to meet the needs of battle. Divisions were divided into three Brigades each with four Battalions of infantry (or, in some cases, cavalry). These Battalions were of course the regimental battalions already mentioned. Divisions had the usual supportive troops — the Divisional Troops. Appendix III gives details of Lines of Communication (L of C), Army Corps and Divisional Troops. Appendix II gives a list of divisional numbers and names.

Within a Division battalions sometimes had names besides the normal number. In the 41st Division, for example, the 122nd Infantry Brigade consisted of four battalions named Bermondsey (12th East Surrey Regiment), 2nd Portsmouth (15th Hampshire Regiment), Lewisham (11th Queen's Own Royal West Kent Regiment) and Arts and Crafts (18th King's Royal Rifle Corps). In the same Division the Field Artillery Brigades bore similar type names, the CLXXXIII being Hampstead and the Divisional Ammunition Column, the West Ham. The names often denoted that the men enlisted in a town as the result of recruiting drives. Careful reading of the many footnotes in Becke (Ref. 34) will trace most names. (See extracts in Figs. 6 and 7 and the definitions in Note 4.)

7

ORDERS OF BATTLE AND ALLOCATIONS

These terms are used for the books and documents which give the organisation of the armies at any point in time. This is a sort of family tree of the Army and just as we draw our trees in several forms, the Army also has many methods of describing who reports to whom.

There appear to be five general sources, of which only one, Becke (Ref. 34), can be obtained through the library loan service. Part of the *Official History*, Becke sets out which Armies, Army Corps and Divisions took part in each of the battles of the War. Each of the 70-odd Divisions is broken down into the Battalions and Divisional Troops (i.e. the Artillery, RE, ASC and RAMC units) which fought with the Divisions. The footnotes enable the researcher to trace the activities of both Battalions and Divisional Troops within a Division during the course of the War. It does not cover L of C, Army, or Corps Troops.

In the Public Record Office Reference Room there is a copy of Brig. E.A. James' book giving details of each Regiment (Ref. 18). The Imperial War Museum Printed Books Library also has a copy. The PRO at Kew has a set of the Orders of Battle issued by the GHQ in France. These are arranged in a different manner to Becke. Each refers to the situation at a specific date, usually at approximately monthly intervals. It gives lists of all GHQ, L of C, Army and Corps Troops as well as the Divisions with which each Battalion fought at that date. It has tables which give the allocation of each unit of the Corps (ASC, RE, RAMC) as well as Artillery. As these allocations changed often during the war, the whole set has to be searched to ensure that a true picture has been obtained.

The Allocation Lists were also issued as separate publications for each Corps and some of these can be found in the PRO and at some Regimental Museums.

Lastly, the index to War Diaries WO95/... on the shelves of the Reference Room at Kew, is in the form of an Order of Battle for October 1918.

Although these sources were republished at intervals, they were not always correct. As an example, the basic unit of ASC transport was the Company. This was attached to a Division to carry supplies from the railhead or other dump up to the divisional supply point. Its full name as obtained from an Allocation List might be 'No. 179 Coy ASC (18th Div. Supply Column)'. However the book on the No.179 Coy ASC written by the Company Sergeant Major says that when the 18th Division moved to another part of the front in 1916, the Supply Column stayed behind and acted as Supply Column for the 34th Div. which took over the front vacated by the 18th, but the name of the Company remained the '18th Div. Supply Column' until 1917 when it was changed to '34th Div. Transport Column' as part of an army transport reorganisation. Such changes are only partly apparent from a study of the Allocation Lists and Orders of Battle.

In general, each Division, its Brigades and Battalions together with the Divisional Troops stayed together throughout the War. However, there were enough exceptions to prevent the researcher basing too many assumptions on this apparent permanency. The following are a few examples.

> The 30th–35th Divisions were disbanded in April 1915 but later reformed (Note 16).
>
> In March 1918 the four Battalions of each Brigade were reduced to three. This meant men were transferred to other Battalions or Brigades. Becke gives details of these moves in many footnotes.
>
> Movements of the Royal Artillery Brigades were very complicated. They were constantly changed with the introduction of new guns and manning arrangements; again Becke gives helpful information.
>
> In March 1916 the Field Ambulance Workshops (ASC units) were absorbed into the Divisional Supply Column. This latter unit, also of the ASC, was part of the Corps Troops but allocated by the Corps to the Division. Many Divisions lost their Cavalry and Cyclist Companies in 1916 and acquired Machine Gun Companies in 1917.

The researcher dealing with a difficult case must be prepared to study changes and movements such as the above in great detail if he is to achieve the desired result.

8

MONTHLY RETURNS

If you have managed to tie the embarkation for France down to a month or two from dated letters, cards, etc., then the Monthly Returns in the PRO (Note 7) will help you trace the ancestor's unit. These returns show where the units of the Army were stationed each month. For home-based units, the town or training depot is given but for the others only the single word *Overseas* or *France* is used. The date when the unit was first posted to the current location is given for home-based units only.

In the *Overseas* section there are often two groups of units, one smaller group will be those units outside Europe, while the other, usually larger, will be marked 'B.E.F.' and refers to France. Lists of exact sailing dates for some corps units are given in WO95/5494.

An examination of the actual date for leaving the UK for those units listed for the first time in the Overseas section shows that they had all sailed by the middle of the previous month, i.e. the June issue did not include units which were sent overseas after about the 15th of May. However, some returns took a long time to appear in print and the same June issue might well include units for the first time who sailed for France before the 15th April and who would normally have been included in the May issue.

By carefully checking through these books, which are bound in 4-monthly volumes, it is possible to estimate the date for the ancestor leaving the UK and also to trace his movements within the UK. This latter point is most important, as War Diaries do not, in general, start until the unit arrives on a foreign shore (but see Note 8). On this point, some of the divisional histories given in A.F. Becke provide further information on UK service but even he had difficulties in finding data for the production of his volume.

For those who still cannot positively identify the exact unit, the date of sailing of several possible units could be compared with known dates from family sources. When the number of possible units has been reduced to a manageable quantity, the War Diaries of these possible units can be examined to reduce the numbers still further. The benefit of the Monthly Returns as opposed to other sources is that the entries are listed by month and by type of unit. It is thus possible to cover several different types of unit with the minimum of search time.

A further list of Embarkation dates for various units is given in WO 162/7 in the PRO at Kew (Note 17).

9

WAR DIARIES

Every unit of Battalion size or greater kept a War Diary The same applies to smaller but self-contained units of the various Corps. Even the Field Ambulance Workshops with a strength of only 20 men kept a War Diary. These are available in the PRO at Kew in WO 95/1 to over 5,000 (Note 8).

The Class List for War Diaries is in three binders under 'WO95'. The second and third binders list the units according to the Order of Battle 1918. This is not the most helpful of arrangements but the first binder has an index for Infantry Battalions and for Artillery Brigades. For other non-infantry units there is a separate manuscript index in a red binder in the Reference Room; Block M — Additional Finding Aids, classes J—WO. The index gives dates for some units. War Diaries did not usually start until arrival on foreign soil whereas other records give a date for leaving the UK. For France this might not be important but for other war zones, the difference in dates could be significant. With the supportive troops the method of indexing makes the search for a particular unit rather time-consuming. It is worth searching WO95/5494 as this has an index by unit number for some Corps. Be warned that some units, due to merging, may have two or more diaries kept in different boxes.

A day's entry could be a single word, e.g. 'Training', or a full page of tightly packed handwritten script detailing the movement of the unit to a new location with full details of the billets, messing and state of the weather. An action could take many pages. Be warned, however, that the names of individual private soldiers seldom appear. Gallantry awards often rate a mention as do unusual offences even if not followed by a Court Martial. NCOs appear more often; whilst practically every officer is named once or twice. It has been noted that some Army Staff Diaries give an official weather report. (2nd Army Director of Medical Services WO95/285.)

Careful reading of the ancestor's unit's Diary is worthwhile for although his name is unlikely to be there, a great deal of background is to be found in its pages. Even information of a true family history nature can be found.

> One entry reports that the officer in charge was on special leave to Ireland to visit his sick mother and another reports the transfer of a man to another unit nearby so that he could be with his brother. In both cases, names were given, which admittedly is rare in the case of other ranks.

Even less likely to give names are the Military HQ Papers for Armies, Corps and Divisions in WO158/... which usually deal with plans for large scale actions.

As War Diaries are the only remaining contemporary source available to the majority of searchers, every effort should be made to extract all the information from them. Not only should the Diary of the ancestor's unit be carefully read but also those of the next echelon up in the Army organisation. If the unit was a Battalion, then check the Brigade and Divisional diaries; if a Corps unit, search the Diary of the responsible Staff Officer at Brigade, Divisional or Corps HQ. It is also rewarding to examine the Diaries of those units who performed their duties in conjunction with the ancestor's unit or who trained or travelled together.

The ancestor's unit, a Motor Ambulance Convoy, arrived in France and was stationed at a small village. The War Diary does not give a precise map reference or details of the billet. However, there is an indirect mention of tents. The Diary of the Deputy Director of Medical Services at Corps HQ to whom the unit reported states that the DDMS visited the site of the MAC giving a map reference and adding that the tents, being pitched in a wood, could not be arranged in a neat military manner. At a later date after a change of location the DDMS reports a visit from the officer in charge of the MAC who complains that his men had been turned out of their billets to make room for an infantry battalion and that they now had insufficient tentage. The DDMS was able to arrange for the supply of 15 rolls of (tarred) felting and wood to construct huts as well as making two bell tents available. No mention was made of these events in the unit's own Diary.

On another occasion, the War Diary reports that two ambulances were lost when the enemy overran the Advanced Dressing Station run by No.36 Field Ambulance (a medical unit, not a vehicle). This is confirmed by a brief description of the event in the official *Medical History*. The official *Military History* also refers to the incident and reports the fall of the village by 8.30 am on 30th November 1917 but makes no reference to medical units.

A search of the Diary of No. 36FA reveals that the pages for November 1917 are missing (were they lost in the action?) but also filed most thoughtfully in the same box is a copy of the history of the FA prepared by the unit historian a few months later. This devotes an entire page to the action and tells how some of the men escaped.

War Diaries of Artillery units are reported to be less helpful. Only Brigades kept Diaries, not the individual Batteries, and these tended only to give the location of Brigade HQ and not the location of the guns. The remoteness of the Batteries from Brigade HQ also precluded any mention of individual men. Frequent changes of location, often at night, was another reason given for poor diaries. None of this makes the task of the researcher any easier when dealing with the constant change of Brigade composition.

10

WAR ESTABLISHMENTS

The War Establishment is a document which gives the number of men supposed to be in a unit with details of the principal equipment, i.e. guns or lorries (see Note 9).

These were published at various times during the War and comparison between them can show how certain units were reduced in strength or combined with others to obtain more effective use of the available manpower. They provide the family historian with a picture of the size and make-up of the ancestor's unit and might give a clue to the type of unit.

For example, if a photo shows the ancestor with a group of 12 men standing in front of a repair workshop, it is comforting to note that the War Establishment of an ASC Workshop was 12 men and one officer.

If you know that an ancestor had a particular job, e.g. an ambulance driver, then a search through the War Establishments would help locate all types of unit that employed ambulance drivers.

War Establishments will also indicate if men of another Corps were attached to the unit.

11

MOBILISATION STORES TABLES

These are of very little value to the family historian but give an interesting side light on the ancestor's unit. They consist of a list of every piece of equipment required by a unit down to the smallest detail. For example, the list for an 800 patient Casualty Clearing Station — a tented hospital — includes

122	Tents or Marquees of 5 types
208	Bedsteads
848	Stretchers
32	Pots, chamber, enamelled
16	Pots, mustard, enamelled
1	Whisk, egg

Plus about 200 more items which made up 40 three-ton lorry loads.

The location of a full set of these is not known, but they may be found in Regimental Museums and perhaps among GHQ papers at Kew. The IWM has about 50 of the forms in Box G of the Army Forms Collection. The Royal Corps of Transport Museum has a similar number but only for ASC units.

12

UNIT EMBLEMS

Most Divisions of the British Armies in France had an emblem which was used to identify lorries and other large items of equipment. Many self-contained Corps units had similar signs. At some stage of the war it is believed that orders were given to paint out these emblems as they could be of use to the enemy.

They can help the researcher in several ways. If they appear in any photographs, they can help to identify the unit. Conversely, if the emblem of the ancestor's unit or its associated division can be found, it can be used to identify the unit in the photographs in the IWM.

Emblems usually take the form of a simple 'heraldic' device or an outline which could be painted with the aid of a stencil. The whereabouts of a list of emblems is not known but mention or a description can sometimes be found in the unit's War Diary. Other sources are the Regimental Museum, unit histories or photographs of known units.

> To quote an example, a search was being made for a picture of the ancestor's unit, No. 24 Motor Ambulance Convoy, in the Photo Library. The War Diary gives a small sketch of the emblem and describes it as an owl in a ring. The Library has only a few photos of MACs but one shows 'No. 24 MAC on the St.Pol–Arras Road Feb. 1916'; a second copy in another book says 'No. 27 MAC'. An obvious mistype from a badly written '4' which is proved by the fact that all the cars have a white owl painted within a ring on the side, and that the HQ of No. 24 at that date was half a mile from the St.Pol–Arras Road. No. 27 was stationed many miles away.

There is a Military Heraldry Society which takes an interest in such matters. Their magazine, *The Formation Sign,* is available in the Imperial War Museum Printed Books Library (Note 15). This could be used to locate an expert on WWI emblems. The Photographic Library has several photographs showing sheets of emblems. One of the longest lists of emblems is the 150-card, two-part, series of cigarette cards given away with Players Cigarettes in the 1920s (Note 22). There is also a book by Mike Chappell, *British Battle Insignia (1) 1914–18* (Ref. 64). WO161/13 at PRO Kew contains a short list of some ASC Emblems. This says that the owl used by No. 24 MAC (see above) was a visual pun on the name of the first CO, Capt. Howlett.

13

RECRUITING

Did the ancestor volunteer or was he conscripted?

Up to July 1915, the Army consisted of 'Regulars', 'Territorials' and fresh volunteers. These latter formed the basis of the so called 'New Armies'. By the middle of 1915 it became clear that the War was going to need a lot of men and that the supply of volunteers was not high enough to keep the planned armies at full strength.

The National Registration Act of July 1915 compelled everyone between 15 and 65 to register. By this means the Government had at its disposal, by September, a breakdown of the population by sex, age and occupation. This showed that a large number of eligible men not engaged in 'starred' occupations (i.e. not engaged in vital war work) were still available. On the 16th October Lord Derby introduced his so-called *Derby Scheme* which allowed men one last chance to enlist voluntarily.

Those who chose not to volunteer at once could attest with the obligation to come forward if called upon. The attested men were then divided into married and single and split into 23 age 'Groups' between 18 and 41. Some 215,000 volunteered for immediate service and a further 2,910,000 attested. The *Derby Scheme* closed on 15th December 1915. A balance of the figures showed over half a million men still evading service, having neither volunteered nor attested. Conscription was, therefore, introduced on 7th January 1916 for all male British subjects aged between 18 (on 5th August 1915) and 41 (on 2nd March 1916) who were unmarried or widowers without a dependent, on 2nd November 1915. Those called up had no choice of unit. There were, of course, exemptions for those unfit and those in the indispensable 'starred' trades. The Act was extended to married men on 25th May 1916. Those conscripted were divided into age 'Classes' (as opposed to 'Groups' used for *Derby* men) between 18 and 41. Single men in Classes 1—23 and married men in Classes 24—46 were born between 1875 and 1897. Actual Call Up dates were as follows.

Derby single men Groups 2–5 (aged 19-22): 25th January 1916 and then in succession up to Group 23 and finally Group 1 on 28th March 1916, at roughly two Groups per week. All conscripted single men were called by Class beginning on 3rd March and finishing on the 25th March. *Derby* married men were called between 7th March and 13th June 1916 and finally all conscripted men between 3rd and 24th June 1916. Due to a number of exemptions, unfitness, etc., compulsion added only a further 43,000 recruits. In general those under 19 (it was changed to 18½ in March 1918, after 3 months training) were not allowed to serve overseas, although there were many who gave false ages. The Army Council Instruction which applied from 1st June 1916 defined five classes, of fitness A, B, C, D and E, the first four being subdivided into three sub-classes, e.g. Class A was 'able to march, see to shoot, hear well and stand active service conditions', B2 was 'able to walk five miles to and from work, see and hear sufficiently for ordinary purposes'. The PRO at Kew has attestation papers in WO96/. . . which for a few regiments extend up to September 1915.

To sum up, if the ancestor was in the Army before September 1915 he was either a Regular, Reservist or a volunteer, be he part-time Territorial called up for full time service or one who answered Kitchener's call. During the period September 1915 to 13th June 1916 it was still possible to have been a volunteer as the pressures to do so were very high. After 2nd March 1916, for single men, and 25th May, for married men, it was not possible to volunteer, although those who had volunteered before those dates could have had their call-up delayed to as late as 13th June. At about this time the Territorial Army was amalgamated with the Regular Army. (See page 150, Vol V, 1916 and page 50, Vol III, 1915 of Ref. 32 for further details.) Men usually had to report for duty one month after their Group or Class was called.

There is a book, *Kitchener's Army,* by Peter Simkins of the Imperial War Museum, which deals with recruiting (Ref. 64).

The time spent in England during training varied but could be as short as a few months. Leave was granted every four or five months plus a period of two or three days before embarkation. The unit then usually left the country two or three days after return from leave.

In the early days of the War, those who enlisted in their local Territorial Regiment had certain advantages. Although full time, the soldier in a Territorial Regiment was more likely to be at a depot near to his home, and evening passes or even sleeping-out passes were available. Volunteers were also more likely to be able to select the Regiment of their own choice rather than being posted by the recruiting officer to a Regiment most in need of men. Men in Territorial Battalions had to specifically volunteer for overseas service so the new recruit could decide to serve at home, although much pressure would be used to encourage him to sign on for overseas service. In general, Territorial Battalions were better equipped and uniformed than the 'Kitchener Battalions'. These advantages disappeared after the first few months of the War.

It appears that each Regiment or Corps had its own sequence of regimental numbers which it issued to soldiers. There was no universal method or sequence used throughout the Army. This meant that if a man changed his Regiment he changed his number. It is worth studying lists of numbers for one Regiment and trying to obtain a connection between number and date of joining. A good starting point would be the volume of *Soldiers Died in the Great War* covering the ancestor's regiment and the National Roll of Honour for the Regiment's 'home town' or area. By comparing the two sources, one could probably estimate the ancestor's date of joining from his number. With the ASC, at least, the prefix letters to the number give a clue to the trade and hence to the type of unit. Ml and M2 were mechanics or fitters. DM was Driver/mechanic, etc. Each type of trade had its own series of numbers. A glance through *Soldiers Died in the Great War* will trace many more prefixes but will not help to identify them.

14

PLACE NAMES AND MAPS

When tracing the ancestor's journeys across France and Belgium, care must be taken not to mistake the places named in various documents. Many of the smaller French villages have similar if not identical names, some only a few miles distant from each other. Some have a second part of the name which differentiates them from their neighbours. This second part is often dropped from entries in War Diaries either from lack of knowledge of its significance or just to save time and space. Often the correct name is given in the initial entry but subsequent entries are only in the shortened form. To quote an example, the village of Aubigny can be found some 10 miles NW of Arras and a second one 10 miles east of Amiens, some 30 miles to the south. The former has an added name of Aubigny-en-Artois but the War Diary of a unit stationed there only gives the full name once. In this case, both villages were near the front line. All this helps to confuse the researcher and care should be taken in checking the location on a map.

Sheet 236 of the Michelin 1/200,000 series (about 3 miles to the inch) covers the whole battle area except, perhaps, the latter days of the War near to the German frontier (Note 18). It shows the location of most of the War Cemeteries. Even better are the very detailed maps and plans given in the *Official History* (Ref. 32) as these are to a very large scale and mention the farms and villages used in the Diaries. They also use English names given to places and locations by the soldiers which will not be found on modern maps, however detailed. The official maps are also useful in that they have in most cases an overprint showing the Armies, Army Corps and Divisions which held a particular part of the Front at a specified date. Unfortunately the maps in the *Official History* do not cover areas behind the line to any great extent. Locations of hospitals and other RAMC units can be found on maps in the *History of Medical Services* (Ref. 29) and transport depots can be found in Ref. 24.

Further maps of the battle area in France, and in other War Zones, can be found in the PRO, Kew, Class WO153/. . . and WO297/. . . (see PRO Record Information Leaflet 115). These maps were originally included with the War Diaries and other records, but were extracted and indexed separately.

Many are overlaid with detailed battle dispositions of troops units, etc. These often mark the location of individual units or the areas where named reserve units were billeted. This latter point is useful as the *Official History* frequently fails to mention these units.

An example of the grid system used on Army maps. Samples can be found in a variety of scales. The numbered squares are 1,000 yds square.

The reference for the bridge over the railway can be expressed in several ways of increasing accuracy, viz. Sheet 57c R8d; 57c R8dSE; 57c R8d 6.4 or 57c R8d 65.45. The last method locates the point to within 25 yards.

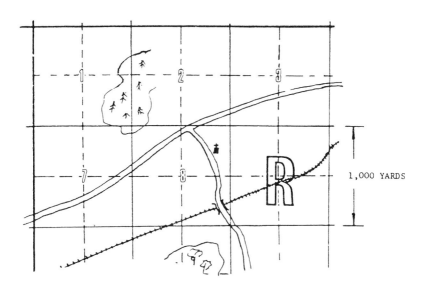

A section of Sheet 57c showing part of the large square R.

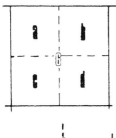

Small square 6 indicating the position of the four lettered sub-divisions. The small letters a, b, c and d do not appear on the map.

The method used to sub-divide the smallest squares. The example reads: 4d 65.45. The graduations do not appear on the map.

The index is arranged in order of the Army, Army Corps and Division from whose records they were extracted, and then by date. (The sequence of numbers is often broken up by other non-related entries. Hence, search all the index to check that you have seen all relevant entries.) Therefore, without knowing the area covered by the Army, Army Corps or Division at the given date, the desired map may be difficult to locate. Other maps can be found within the War Diaries of the Staff Officers of Army Corps and Armies as these appear to have missed the extraction procedure. Some are also included in the HQ Papers of Divisions, Army Corps and Armies in WO158/. . . This latter class is very patchy, some units being well covered and others having no records at all.

Within War Diaries, place names were frequently given map references. These are in the form *Sheet 62D E17a.* These refer to a series of maps to a scale of approx. 1/20,000 or 5cm to 1 kilometre (3 inches/mile). The entire battle area was divided into large rectangles each allocated a capital letter (the 'E' in *E17a*); this rectangle was divided into approximately 30 squares each representing an area of about 1,000 yards by 1,000 yards (some lettered rectangles were divided into 36 squares). Each square was given a number, shown in the centre of the rectangle (the '17'). The 1,000 yard squares are again divided into four 500 yard squares by 2 dotted lines and designated a, b, c, d. The exact point within the 500 yard square was sometimes defined by adding a compass point or position as *E17a central* or *E17aNW.* At this scale the battle covered a large map area so for convenience the grid is divided into numbered sheets. The PRO Map Room at Kew does not hold a complete set of these maps but the sheet required may be found within the collections in WO153/. . . mentioned above, but the sheet numbers do not appear in the index. Maps are not ordered on the computer terminals but by 'manual' slips presented at the map room counter on the 2nd floor. Waiting time is usually only one or two minutes.

During the last few years a collection of large scale maps, known as *Trench Maps,* have been released. They are held in the PRO at Kew under WO 297/...

As an example of the use of detailed maps, consider the photograph in the Imperial War Museum (not reproduced) which shows 'an Advanced Dressing Station on the Montouban-Guillemont Road in September 1916 — showing in addition, two lorries of the 16th Div. (Irish) with Shamrocks on the side'. Volume IV of the *Official History* which covers the fighting on the Somme in great detail has a map of a scale of about four or five inches to the mile, which shows the road connecting the two villages. One part of this road is shown tree lined. The stumps of the trees can be seen lining the section of road visible in the photo. Reading the text one can find that the 16th Div. joined the fighting on the 3rd September and left the front on the 9th September. It would not be until the battle had passed over the village on the 5th or 6th that an ADS would be at that position. Hence one can tie the place and date down very closely. In fact the modern Michelin maps show a War Cemetery on the exact spot. It's a sad fact that many men died when help was at hand. A closer look at the photo shows at least one grave already marked in the mud. The *Official History* records show that the 16th lost over 4,000 men during those few days, over 20% of whom would have been killed.

The knowledge of the map reference is of greater importance than is at first obvious as it is used to find aerial photographs in the Imperial War Museum Photograph Library. They have a very large collection showing areas of ground up to 1 mile square but often much smaller. The negatives are filed by year; Sheet No.; Reference; date taken. Using this index, it is possible to find a bird's eye view of the ancestor's camp taken during the time that he was there.

15

LOCATION OF SOURCES

Having outlined the contents of documents such as Monthly Returns, Orders of Battle, Allocation Lists and War Diaries, the problem is where to find them. The PRO at Kew has most of the information but it is sometimes difficult to locate. As explained, the Index to WO 95 (War Diaries) is in the form of an Order of Battle, but unless you know the Army, Army Corps or Division with which the ancestor's unit was associated, it means searching through two volumes of the index. Regiments and Artillery are easier to find as they are listed by Regiment, Battalions and Brigades at the beginning of the first volume.

It is well worthwhile checking WO95/5467–70 and WO95/5494. The former contains Orders of Battle for various periods throughout the War and these often have a partial index to units. The latter is a collection of lists, some manuscript and heavily annotated, which give details of Unit Allocation, Changes of Unit Allocation, Locations and Postings indexed by Location and Unit. For some Corps there is an index of War Diaries arranged in Unit number order (see Notes 5 and 8).

The Imperial War Museum has separate Libraries for Printed Books, Manuscripts, Photographs and Pictures. Entrance can be obtained by telephoned appointment — three or four days' notice. The Printed Book Library will have a selection of books awaiting you if you explain your requirements even in general terms, e.g. 'any histories dealing with the Bedfordshire Regiment'. They hold copies of Becke and GHQ Staff Order of Battle for two dates. They also hold most of the published unit histories as well as copies of Regimental Journals and Magazines.

The Photographic Library has over 5,000,000 pictures for both World Wars of which 100,000 date from WWI. Besides being card indexed for town, unit number or name, type of unit, man's name (really only applies to senior officers!) and type of subject, they have hundreds of albums lining the wall where the indexed photos can be viewed. Another section of the albums has the same set of pictures filed according to subject matter. This is well cross-indexed. It's a long shot but you might find a picture of the ancestor's unit showing the ancestor. The collection is still being added to at the rate of 50,000 per year (not all from WWI) but the recent additions are not as well indexed due to staff shortages This is unfortunate as many photos from old soldiers are now coming to light. Experience has shown that the captions are sometimes inaccurate or incomplete so try to check the photo against a map or unit War Diary to ensure you have made the correct selection.

Copies of photos can be obtained at a modest price.

The Manuscript Library has many private diaries indexed by unit and unit type. Others can be located with the aid of Ref. 3.

Most Regiments and Corps have a Regimental Museum and Library. Some, like the Royal Artillery, have a Historical Society. The quality of the material in libraries varies but it usually includes a set of printed unit histories of the Regiment and often much manuscript data. Unfortunately, the curator is often doing it as a part-time job and may not know the value of the records to family history researchers. If you can get inside the record room, you may strike lucky. Some Regiments still have lists of pre-War Regulars who served throughout the War. They also kept many old photos of groups of men taken at sports events and passing out parades. A number of books (Refs. 15 and 16) will enable you to locate the museum associated with the ancestor's unit.

Your local library can usually get any of the books so far mentioned through the inter-library service but it can take several weeks. The Reference shelves often have the standard series of Regimental Histories and books of badges, etc. (Refs. 39—44.)

The Guildhall Library also has a collection of *Lloyd's Registers of Shipping* which can be a help in identifying the ship used by the ancestor for the trip across the Channel or, for that matter, to any other war zone. The name of the ship is often given in the War Diary; if not, check the Diaries of those units who went overseas on the same day and who record the same ports of departure and arrival and similar times in their Diaries. It often happens that one of these latter documents will list the ship or give other information. Details of the ships are to be found in one of the numerous books on early steam ships (Refs. 54—60). They were usually cross- channel or other ferry boats taken over for the duration of the war by the Admiralty. Canadian cattle boats were often used for horses and other transport.

16

BOOKS

Many books have been written about the Great War but only some are of use to the family historian. The 'official' Regiment or Corps Histories often go into great detail and individual companies or units may be mentioned. When dealing with Corps this is probably the only place you will find any reference to the ancestor's unit. The Corps or Regimental Journal or Magazine often gives an article on a certain type of unit. This is well worth searching for if the type of unit is unusual, as it will probably be the only description available.

For a non-political detailed history of the war, which deals in facts and figures, the *Official History of the War* in 14 volumes is excellent, but difficult to obtain as very few libraries seem to have it and it has a complicated numbering system. With it, one can trace the path of individual Battalions or, in some cases, even Companies. Chapters IV to VI (1916 to 1st July) give a very good description of all the types of unit within the Army. In all cases the text concentrates on the main battles and on units in the Front Line. During the time a unit was resting, no mention is made of it, not even the fact that it was resting.

The activities of other Corps can be checked in the remaining books of the Series as listed in Government Publications Sectional List No. 60.

Many of the more well-known histories deal with politics and strategy and the family historian will find little of interest. The three bibliographies listed (Refs. 1–3) give numerous books written by soldiers and provide plenty of background information on life in the trenches.

Some of the unit histories listed in Enser and in White (Refs. 1 and 2) may be difficult to find, but they are very worthwhile trying to locate, even if it means a visit to the Imperial War Museum Library, as they often give a complete roll of the men who served in the unit. This will probably be the only confirmation available. The bibliography which follows (pp. 47–54) is by no means complete but it lists a few books which should be of use to the family historian. Standard bibliographies such as White or Enser run to several hundred pages each.

Once you have discovered the ancestor's unit, check the various units that served with it. In this way you will build up a complete picture of all Corps units and Battalions who fought with him. Using this list, look up each of the separate units by name and number in the various bibliographies and indexes. In this way you might find a book written on, for example, the Field Ambulance attached to the ancestor's Battalion.

Don't forget the local newspaper. These usually published the list of wounded local men as well as the occasional news item on men serving overseas. Deaths usually rated a picture and a short report, often with extracts from the CO's letter to the next-of-kin. Men mentioned in despatches and given other awards also got a paragraph with, in most cases, a photograph. These, too, often give details of the circumstances of the award, facts that are not available elsewhere. Finding the item can be time-consuming but rewarding. Official advertisements and reports gave lists of men who had failed to answer to their call-up papers and proceedings of the Tribunals to consider exemption from call-up. These latter sometimes did not give names but in a small village the men could be identified by the other details published. See Note 22 for Quakers.

17

USING PHOTOGRAPHS

Many families will still have in their possession photographs of the ancestor in uniform and perhaps others showing a group of men, including the ancestor. These can be of great use to the researcher. Besides the obvious method of identification of the Corps or Regiment from badges and other insignia there is a method of proving that the photograph in fact shows what it purports to show.

It will often be the case that, after a long search, the ancestor's unit will be deduced from the known facts. A unit will be found that meets all the requirements of date and location but nowhere can a list of names be found that will offer conclusive proof that the ancestor served with that unit. By looking carefully at the picture, see if there are any officers, senior NCOs or medal ribbon wearers visible. Can the picture be dated even roughly by service and/or good conduct stripes? The next step is to read the War Diary of the unit selected as being that of the ancestor, and which hopefully is the one depicted in the group photograph. Make a list of the names of all officers, NCOs and medal recipients mentioned in the diary. From this it should be possible to put names to at least some of those shown in the photo, taking into account the likely date on which it was taken. Now select the man with the most unusual name and try to find him in the births index at the Family Records Centre. With medal holders a check should be first made from the *London Gazette* entry as this will give the home town and thus aid the location of the correct reference. If the name is rare the family can usually be located by a few telephone calls to the entries in the phone directory covering the 'places of birth' found from the Family Records Centre or the *London Gazette.*

Should the name be more common, a search should be made to find the marriage and, as the indexes give the wife's maiden name after the end of 1911 and also births give the mother's maiden name from September 1911, the children of that marriage can be located. If the full names of any male children are noted, it should be easy to contact them as they may still be alive. Armed with a list of possible men, marriages and male children, pay a visit to the Guildhall Library and search back. Telephone Directories, Town Directories and, for medal holders, the *London Gazette:* all these books are there and the library is open on Saturdays.

Having located your contact, first confirm that he is a descendant of the right man, i.e. his father did serve in that unit, did win that medal or has the right army number. Then send him a copy of your photograph. With luck, he will spot his ancestor standing next to yours in the same picture. This proves that, at the time the photograph was taken, both men were together, most likely in the same unit, and as you know the unit of one of the men because his name is in the War Diary, the other man, your ancestor, must also have been in the same unit.

It will be noted that the man contacted does not have to know his ancestor's unit. He only has to identify him in a photo and most people can do this even if the soldier was only 20 years old at the time the picture was taken. In case of non-identification, repeat the process with another name. Failure to obtain an identification does not mean you have the wrong unit, only that the man you have selected from the War Diary was not there when the picture was taken.

18

ARMY LIFE IN FRANCE

To obtain an insight into the life of a soldier it is best to read several of the many published soldiers' diaries or compilations of war experiences. However, the family historian might be interested in the following points.

Before 1st March 1916, when volunteering was stopped, a man could join the Regiment of his choice, if they would accept him. He could thus travel to the recruiting centre of the Regiment, usually in a town in the area bearing the Regiment's name, and enlist. If he preferred, he could enlist with his father's 'old Regiment' or one associated with his own 'home town'. Alternatively, he could choose one of the Corps, e.g. ASC or RE, especially if he had a trade, as they often paid more. The ordinary soldier was paid one shilling a day while certain skilled men could earn six shillings a day.

After 1916 men enlisted anywhere and were posted according to their skills and the requirements of the Army.

Once enlisted, training began and took several months although at times of great need it was made shorter. No leave would be granted for a period of at least 10-15 weeks although an evening pass to visit a nearby town could be obtained. After that, men were released in turn to go on leave every 20-odd weeks. In most cases this meant no leave before the time came to sail for France. It was then usual to grant 48 or 72 hours leave to the whole unit. Upon return from leave four days were spent packing, etc. and by the fifth day the unit was on the way to the Port. If a complete Division was assembled in England it was customary for the King to inspect it before sailing – see Becke (Ref. 34).

A man could go to France as part of a complete unit, i.e. a Battalion or ASC Company, or as part of a draft, which was a group of men who would be allocated to another unit or units once in France. On the other side of the Channel a short stay would be made at a large transit camp. Here the completed units could wait until all the men and vehicles had crossed before proceeding further. The drafts would wait until their final destination was determined, then they would be given the appropriate cap badges and sent up to the line to join their unit.

It can be seen that already the ancestor might have changed Regiment or, more commonly, his Battalion.

Transport to the Front Line would be by train and finally by marching. Mechanised units could use their own vehicles. Up to 1916, when Nissen huts began to be introduced, men stationed behind the line such as Transport, Medical and Supply units would live in barns or tents. Officers would be billeted in a house. Beds or bunks were unknown, the men sleeping on the ground or on straw. Within a short time everyone was covered with lice and fleas which could not be got rid of until the return to England.

When one was stationed nearer the front, shell fire forced the men into dugouts in the ground or into cellars of ruined houses. Gun crews were often subject to enemy fire and hence they also lived in dugouts. In certain areas movement on the roads, if any were left, brought an immediate hail of shells. Hence, all work tended to be done at night.

For the fighting men in the Front Line, the situation was much worse. Each unit would spend a period in the first line trench. This entailed leaving most of their kit behind at the transport area perhaps two or three miles behind the front. Then, encumbered with extra ammunition, hand grenades, entrenching tools and other items for survival, often weighing 60–70 pounds, they would march forward at night to take over the trench within 50–300 yards of the German lines. The last mile or more of the approach might itself be along a communication trench, knee deep in water. Once in the Front Line trench they would have to stay there day and night till relieved in 4–15 days. At times they had to 'stand-to', i.e. stand up on a raised 'shelf' (the firing step) in the trench ready to shoot over no-man's-land. At other times they could 'stand down' or in other words stay at the bottom of the trench often deep in mud. To sleep they took it in turns to crawl into narrow recesses scooped out of the sides of the trench. When relieved they retired to a second line perhaps 100–200 yards to the rear where living conditions were a little better. Here they were often called upon at night to come forward, past the Front Line, into no-man's-land to put up barbed wire defences or to help rebuild trenches damaged by shell fire. Food for both lines would be brought up by fatigue parties from the cooks stationed near the transport. This often took two to three hours due to the mud and shell fire.

Their turn of duty in the trenches finished, the unit would retire to the rear area and try to relax although they still had to sleep in dugouts and cellars as they were within shelling range. Nights were spent moving supplies to the Front Line from rearward depots or providing working parties to repair or make roads and railways. After a week or 10 days the cycle would repeat itself. With luck they might have been able to visit a bath house during this time where they could have a hot bath or shower and a change of underwear; however, the fleas always survived the cleaning.

After one or two months the whole unit would withdraw several miles, usually beyond shelling range. Here they could rest, train and help with transport and repairs. With luck they could live in barns, etc. above ground and move freely at all times. The whole cycle would repeat itself again after about a month.

At less frequent intervals, the Division and then the Corps would be withdrawn into reserve so that all units contained within them could enjoy a period well away from the front. The time was spent in training or rehearsing new attacks.

Most of the time in the Front Line trench was spent watching; occasionally a small raid would be made on the enemy to capture a prisoner. The total length of the famous named battles took only about one third of all the time between 1914 and 1918. Hence, on any one stretch of front, battles were comparatively rare. Some parts were inactive right up to the last three months of the war. However, units were switched from one part to another so that 'fresh' troops could be used in a heavy attack. Units of fighting troops involved in an attack could lose 50% of their strength in killed and wounded. In some cases it was even more. The numbers would be made up with fresh drafts of men from England. No records of the names of these latter still exist.

The men of the various Corps represented about one third to a half of the total army strength and those units allocated as Divisional Troops had a more dangerous time than Corps, Army or Lines of Communication Troops.

Divisional Artillery was often under shell fire from the opposing side; Royal Engineers Signal sections would frequently have to lay or repair telephone cables in sight of the enemy and Companies of Royal Engineers would work in no-man's-land laying barbed wire. However, during their non-working periods they could retire to the comparative safety of a dug-out or billet in a cellar a mile or two behind the line.

Life would continue like this seven days a week, 52 weeks a year until home leave was granted. This would be about 10 or 14 days, including travelling time, every 12 months or so. For officers at least, they could choose to take their leave in the South of France (Note 13).

At the end of the war, men were demobilised from about December 1918 onwards. Men in important industries, like miners, were released first; followed in order by others of lower priority. Most men were home by May or June 1919 except those forming the Army of the Rhine.

19

RESEARCH METHODS

These depend to a large extent on what the researcher aims to achieve, but the research can usually be split into several phases. First the tracing of the exact unit in which the ancestor served; then the obtaining of background information on the history of that unit in relation to a general knowledge of what took place during the war. Finally, an attempt could be made to find evidence of the ancestor's service. Perhaps a photograph could be found in the archives or a mention of his name in one of the few extant documents.

The most difficult step is the first, that is to find the unit. Those who have family evidence which gives precise details will have saved themselves a great deal of trouble. For those not in this fortunate position, the procedure is as follows.

First of all, make out a list of all the known facts and unsubstantiated data on the ancestor's career (Fig.1 shows a typical list). Try to put everything down in writing before any deductions are made or research is done, as this will prevent the twisting of the truth in order to make the ancestor's history fit the research findings – a trap into which it is very easy to fall and which completely misleads the researcher. The aim is to find a unit which matches the list in every respect.

With 'Regimental' ancestors use the two bibliographies given in the Reference Section to find a detailed history of the Regiment during the War. In most cases this will provide enough facts to tie the unit down to one Battalion. Failing this a search will have to be made using Becke or one or more volumes of the *Official History*. Problems arise if no one Battalion matches all the data on the list. This often indicates a transfer to another unit. Becke may give a hint in this respect as he gives dates of mergers and disbandments.

Other warning signs of a change of unit are the presence of the ancestor back in England after a period abroad or knowledge of his being wounded. It was common practice for men returning to France after wounding to be posted to the Labour Corps. Also, does the date of leaving England (if known) correspond to the departure date of the Battalion. If not it could mean a transfer to another Battalion while waiting in the Base Camp in France.

Once the Battalion has been identified, it is well worth making a list of every village and town at which it was stationed; also a list of each Division, Corps or Army in which it served. These lists should include dates. The information can be obtained from books and War Diaries. Using these lists, check each item in the indexes in the Imperial War Museum Photograph Library. It is possible, though not likely, that the ancestor appears on a photograph. The Imperial War Museum has over 100,000 photos of WWI — if each shows only 10 men, that is one million or a fifth of all the men who served in France. A one in five chance is well worth a search. The same lists of locations can be used to find diaries in the Imperial War Museum Library or books from the Bibliographies. In this way it is possible to check small details of the ancestor's story.

> Approximately 32 Motor Ambulance Convoys served in France. The Imperial War Museum Photograph Library has pictures of four of these. No. 22 is shown in a series of 10 pictures, a large number of officers and men are visible. Some men are also to be seen in a picture of a second unit.

With Corps or Royal Artillery ancestors, the task is usually more difficult. Not only is the family data less likely to give the unit identification but the number of units is far higher. The best chance of success lies with having enough data to identify the type of unit. Even chance remarks such as, 'He always said that he caught his rheumatism lying on his back on the wet ground repairing lorries', will go a long way towards finding the unit. Once again this should be on the data sheet before a serious start is made on your research.

By studying Corps histories some idea of the variety and types of units should be obtained. The next step would be to compile lists of all suitable units of the Corps which were in the same area as the ancestor at the correct dates. These can be drawn up by reference to the Monthly Returns (for first date in France), GHQ Orders of Battle and War Diaries.

It is best to include all units which served with the Army covering the ancestor's location at that time. The Army boundaries can be found in general histories and Corps histories but they changed frequently and due account of this fact should be taken when compiling the list. In addition, those Lines of Communication and GHQ Troops serving in an Army area should be included. If the Order of Battle does not give this information, then they should all be included until they can be eliminated by reference to the individual War Diaries which of course give the precise location at any date. The list can contain 50 or 70 units but if further lists can be drawn up for two or more dates and corresponding locations of the ancestor, the researcher will find that only a few units appear in all lists. This brings the number down to a manageable size and the War Diaries of these few can be studied to see if any clues can be found to make a more positive identification of the ancestor's unit. (See Fig 2.)

When a possible unit has been identified, proof may be very difficult, as very few lists of men remain. As with Regiments a complete list of dates and locations of the unit should be made and these checked in the indexes of the Imperial War Museum. The chances of finding books or diaries by a member of the unit are probably smaller than with a soldier serving in a battalion as the number of men per unit is somewhat less than the battalion's 1,000. However, the proportion of names being mentioned in the War Diary is somewhat higher as the officer-in-charge would know each man by name.

The War Diaries of units which served alongside the ancestor's should always be examined as they can give extra information.

> The ancestor's unit was stated in the War Diaries to have arrived at Rouen at 5 pm on 18th March 1916 but the name of the ship is not mentioned. While drawing up the list of units which sailed for France within the defined period, it was noticed that two similar units sailed on the same day. The War Diaries of these two units were checked and one recorded that the unit also arrived at Rouen at 5 pm on 18th March 1916 and gave the name of the ship. In addition all three diaries reported that the date for leaving the Base Depot in London was postponed for four days but only one reported the fact that four inches of snow fell overnight before the original departure date, thus making the task of driving 50 ambulances to Avonmouth almost impossible.

Some units contained men from two Corps, for example a heavy artillery battery would be made up of the gun crews from the Royal Artillery and transport drivers and mechanics from the Army Service Corps. In these cases, it is wise to check records in both Corps Museums. War Establishments (q.v., page 24) will give details of this double manning.

> The ancestor served with a Motor Ambulance Convoy which was an RAMC unit although most of the men were from the ASC. The RAMC Museum had very few records on MACs of any description but the ASC Museum was able to produce a three-page history of the ancestor's unit written by the Second in Command, an ASC Captain.

A great deal of effort was expended in making camp sites and dugouts as comfortable as possible, hence when a unit was posted elsewhere, the unit taking over its duties usually took over its camp site and other facilities. Sometimes the unit's War Diary mentions the previous occupant of the site but in any case it is worth checking which unit preceded or succeeded the ancestor's unit and searching its War Diary as well as this will add details of the site conditions.

20

REFERENCE SECTION

20.1 MISSING DOCUMENTS

Besides the main personnel records already mentioned in the chapter on Records, the following items have been lost or destroyed or at least the author has not been able to locate them.

(a) Pay Lists, Muster Rolls, etc.

(b) Orders of unit commanders to subordinate units.

Orders of unit commanders to their own units.

Part I and Part II orders.

Some orders of the larger units, i.e. Corps and Armies, still exist and are to be found attached to War Diaries, either that of the originating unit or that of the recipient. Again HQ Papers on Corps, Armies and Divisions WO 158/... have a few. These tend to be confined to plans for big attacks rather than mundane day to day matters.

(c) Courts Martial Papers **for those who were executed** during WWI (any others were destroyed in the 1940 bombing) are open for inspection but have recently been requisitioned back to the Ministry of Defence. However, lists giving names appear in WO93/49 (death sentences carried out in the British Army during WWI), WO93/42–5 (nominal rolls of courts martial of all ranks of Australian and Canadian forces 1915–9), WO86/..., WO88/..., WO90/..., WO92/... and WO213/... See PRO Leaflet No.84 *Records of Courts Martial; Army.*

(d) Embarkation Lists – may exist for zones other than France but even then only likely to mention officer i/c draft.

(e) Casualty Return Slips or Counterfoils. Admission books for a few military medical units survive in PRO Kew MH106/...

(f) Memos between various units. Sometimes an interesting report or memo may have been attached to the War Diary; but this is an exception rather than the rule.

(g) Unless mentioned in the War Diary or the *London Gazette,* no citations are available for Mentions in Despatches or Military Medals.

(h) All unit orders giving details of transfers, leave applications, promotions have been lost.

(i) A complete list of those wounded before July 1917.

(j) A set of Mobilisation Stores Tables.

20.2 BIBLIOGRAPHY

Dewey Index Numbers for World War 1 are

940.400 General History
940.4144 General Description of Fighting
940.42 Battles
940.465 War Graves
940.48141 War Diaries of Soldiers
355.00941 Military Museums
355.10 Daily Life of Soldiers
355.134 Badges
355.14 Uniform
355.31 } Unit Histories
356.11 }

(1) *A Subject Bibliography of the First World War.* A.G.S. Enser. (Andre Deutsch.) Lists books by subject, town name, battle name, unit name and unit type.

(2) *A Bibliography of Regimental Histories.* A.S. White. Deals with all times, not just WWI. Indexed by Regiment and Corps names.

Some of the books listed in the above books may have been published privately by Regiments and units. Copies may only exist in the Imperial War Museum Library or the Regimental Museum.

(3) *Two World Wars – a Guide to Manuscript Collections in the UK.* S.L. Mayer and W.J. Koenig. (Bowker, London 1976.) A copy is a available on the reference shelves at PRO Kew.

(4) *A Guide to Sources of British Military History.* Robin Higham.

(5) *Army Ancestors.* John W. Brooks. Vol 6 No 1 Summer 1980, Berkshire FHS Journal. A three-page list of sources for the period 1760–1900. Most of the documents listed do not extend later than 1908 and those which do have been covered in this current volume.

(6) *Family History Sources: The Two World Wars.* Clive Vaisey. Vol 2 No 3 July 1981, Journal of NW Kent FHS. Mentions St. Catherine's Indexes, War Graves Commission and War Diaries.

(7) *Army Records: Tracing my Grandfather.* Jean Allen. Vol I No 8 October 1980, Journal of NW Kent FHS. Gives an example of records from Army Search, Hayes.

(8) *In Search of Army Ancestry.* G. Hamilton-Edwards. Pre-1914 only.

(9) Public Record Office Leaflet No 59, *British Military Records as Sources of Biography and Genealogy.*

(10) *Tracing your Ancestors in the Public Record Office.* Amanda Bevan and Andrea Duncan. Fourth Edition, London HMSO. ISBN 0 11 440222 1. Section 18.31 deals with records after 1913 and mentions pensions records in PMG 9, PMG 42, PMG 11 and PMG 44 to 47. A few deaths are listed in RG 35/45 to 69.

(11) PRO Leaflet No 40, *Operational Records of the British Army in the Great War 1914–19.*

(12) *Finding the Men who Fought in the Trenches.* Norman Holding. *Family Tree Magazine,* Vol 2 No 6 (Sept/Oct 1986) and Vol 3 No 1 (Nov 1986). Two articles dealing with research methods.

(13) *History of the First World War.* B.G. Liddel Hart. (Pan Books, 1972.) First published circa 1933. A one-volume general history full of strategy and politics.

(14) *Field Marshal Haig's Despatches.* Edited by John Terraine. Published after the War with a commentary. Makes a very readable factual account of the War from December 1915 to 1918. Not too much politics and a fair amount of detail of the battles and units concerned. If you can't get the *Official History* with its 14 volumes, this is a good substitute, but does not start until December 1915.

(15) *A Register of the Regiments and Corps of the British Army.* Arthur Swinson. (Archive Press, London.) This gives a brief history of the units and enables you to identify the modern successor to the WW1 unit.

(16) *A Guide to Military Museums.* Compiled by Terence Wise. 8th edn. 1994. (Imperial Press.) This gives the location of Military Museums by their modern names.

(17) *Army Service Records of the First World War.* Simon Fowler, William Spencer and Stuart Tamblin. PRO Publications, 1996. Gives full details of both 'Burnt' and 'Unburnt Docs' together with examples.

(18) *British Regiments 1914–18.* Brig. E.A. James. (Samson Books, 1978.) This is a reprint in one volume of two earlier books by the same author dealing with Infantry and Cavalry Regiments. It can be found on open shelves in the Imperial War Museum and the Public Record Office, Kew.

(19) *Discovering British Cavalry Regiments.* Arthur Taylor. (Shire Publications Limited.) Only a very slim book, included because it is often sold on Family History Society bookstalls.

(20) *Locations of British Cavalry, Infantry and Machine Gun Units 1914–1924.* Robert W. Gould MBE.

(21) *Famous Regiments.* Edited by Lt.-Gen. Sir Brian Horrocks. (Leo Cooper Ltd., London.) About 50 volumes covering most of the Regiments and Corps — found in most Libraries but they are not usually detailed enough.

(22) *Royal Army Service Corps – A History of Transport and Supply in the British Army.* Vol 2. Col. R.H. Beadon. (Cambridge University Press, 1930.) This volume deals with the Great War.

(23) A history of various ASC UK depots is given in WO161/30, WO161/12 and 13 and WO95/5466.

(24) *Transportation on the Western Front 1914–18.* Col. A.M. Henniker. One volume plus separate box of maps. This deals with Railway, Road and Vehicle transport. Only of value to those having ancestors in the ASC, RE and RAOC.

(25) *The Work of the Royal Engineers in the European War 1914–18.* The R.E.

Institution 1921–27. Chatham, Kent. Includes volumes on the Signal Service and Water.

(26) *History of the Corps of Royal Engineers.* Vol 5. Brig.-Gen. W. Baker Brown. Published 1952, 728 pages. Covers The Home Front – France Flanders and Italy in the First World War. Vol 6 covers activities in the Middle East 1914–1919.

(27) *History of the Ordnance Services.* Maj.-Gen. A. Forbes. (Medici Society, London, 1929.)

(28) *The Great War and the R.A.M.C.* F.S.Brereton. (Constable, London, 1919.) Goes into real detail but only deals with first two or three months of the War. Vol 1 was the only one published.

(29) *Medical History of the Great War. General History.* Maj.-Gen. Sir W.G. MacPherson in four volumes. Vol 1 Medical Services in UK and African campaigns; Vol 2 Medical Services on the Western Front 1914–15 (includes descriptions of all types of RAMC unit); Vol 3 Medical Services on the Western Front 1916, 1917, 1918 and Italy (includes allocations of RAMC units); Vol 4 Medical Services in Gallipoli, Macedonia, Mesopotamia, North-west Persia, Aden, East Africa and North Russia. Also Ambulance Transport during the War. (A summary of types of vehicles and stretchers.)

(30) *Veterinary Services.* Maj.-Gen. Sir L. J. Blenkinsop and Lt.-Col. J.W. Ramsey. One volume. With (29), would be of interest to those investigating men who served with the ASC Ambulance Convoys, RAMC and Veterinary Units.

(31) Government Publications Sectional List No 60. HMSO. Includes a long list of books published by HMSO. Most are in the series *History of the Great War Based on Official Documents by Direction of the Historical Section of the Committee of Imperial Defence* (examples given in Nos 29, 32, 34, 35), often known simply as the *Official History.* Another list of the *Official History* will be found in *Stand To!,* No.20 Summer 1990 (The journal of the Western Front Association).

(32) The *Official History* is divided into several groups of volumes of which *Military Operations* forms a part. *France and Belgium* has 14 vols. mainly written by Brig.-Gen. Sir James E. Edmonds.

Dates of publication cover the period 1922–1949. In recent years a number of volumes have been re-published, some without the map volume that accompanied the first edition. Further editions of some of the volumes will shortly be published by the Imperial War Museum.

France and Belgium. All by Brig.-Gen. Sir James E. Edmonds unless otherwise stated.

1914 Vol 1 *1914 August–October. Mons, the Retreat to the Seine, the Marne and the Aisne.* With a case of maps. Editions 1922, 1925, 1934. The 1934 edition was reprinted by Shearer Publications in 1984.

1914 Vol 2 *1914 October–November. Antwerp, La Bassee, Armentieres, Messines and Ypres.* With a case of maps. 1925.

1915 Vol 1 (with Capt. G. C. Wynne). *Winter 1914–15. Neuve Chapelle-Ypres, December 1914–May 1915.* With a case of maps. 1927.

1915 Vol 2 *Aubers Ridge, Festubert and Loos.* With a case of maps. 1928.

1916 Vol 1 *1916 to July 1. The Somme.* With a case of maps. 1927. Reprinted by Shearer Publications in 1986.

1916 Vol 1 *Appendices Volume,* 1927.

1916 Vol. 2 *1916, July 2 to End of Somme Battle.* With a case of maps and Appendices.

1917 Vol 1 (Capt. Cyril Falls) *The German Retreat to the Hindenburg Line and the Arras Battles.* With a case of maps and separate volume of Appendices, 1940.

1917 Vol 2 *June 7–November 10. Messines and Third Ypres (Passchendaele).* 1949.

1917 Vol 3 (Capt. W. Mills) *The Battle of Cambrai.* 1949.

1918 Vol 1 *March Offensive.* With a case of maps and separate volume of Appendices. 1935.

1918 Vol 2 *March–April.* With a case of maps. 1937.

1918 Vol 3 *May–July.* 1939.

1918 Vol 4 *August 8–September 28. Franco-British Offensive.* 1947.

1918 Vol 5 *September 28–November 10.* 1947.

There are also volumes for East Africa (1), Egypt and Palestine (2), Gallipoli (2), Italy (1), Macedonia (2), Mesopotamia (4), Togoland and the Cameroons (1) and Persia (1).

The occupation of Germany in 1919 is covered by Brig.-Gen. Sir James E. Edmonds in *The Occupation of the Rhineland 1918–1929.* This was only published in draft form which is in the PRO, Kew (CAB 44/. . . or CAB 45/. . .). However, this was published by the Imperial War Museum in 1988.

When you know your ancestor's unit and something about its battles, this series is a must — it goes into great detail. Chapters IV to VI of France and Belgium 1916 Vol 1, *1916 to July 1st. The Somme,* gives an overall picture of the make-up of the British Army in 1916 right down to the Army Typewriter Service and the Rubber Stamp Factory. Page 12 in 1915 Vol. 1 has a list of Army Schools.

(33) *Order of Battle of British Armies in France.* Gen. Staff GHQ, published many times during the War (about monthly?). There are two issues in Imperial War Museum library. Others are in Regimental Museums. There is a complete set (?) in PRO Kew WO95/5467–5470. This book gives a sort of organisational family tree of the Army in France. It gives far more detail about allocated units than Becke but does not relate units to Battles. Shows the situation at the date of the issue. Enables the tracing of units not given in Becke (Ref. 34), i.e. Lines of Communication, Army and Corps Troops (see also Note 6). The issue for 11th November 1918 has been published by Imperial War Museum February 1989 (ISBN 0 90 1627 49 6).

(34) *Order of Battle of Divisions.* Compiled by Major A.F. Becke. (London, HMSO, 1945.) In 4 parts, parts 2 and 3 each requiring 2 volumes.

Part 1. The Regular British Divisions (1st—9th).

Part 2a. The Territorial Force, Mounted Divisions and 1st Line Territorial Force Divisions (42nd—56th).

Part 2b.   The 2nd Line Territorial Force Divisions (57th—69th) plus the Home Service Divisions (71st—73rd) and the 74th and 75th Divisions.

Part 3a The New Army Divisions (9th—26th).

Part 3b The New Army Divisions (30th—41st) and 63rd (RN) Division.

Part 4 The Army Council, GHQ's Armies and Corps, 1914—1918.

These volumes have been reprinted as follows: Part 1 Sherwood Press 1986; Part 2a Sherwood Press 1987; Part 2b Westlake Military Books 1988; Parts 3a and 3b in one volume by Westlake Military Books 1989.

The above books give a brief history of each Army, Corps or Division, together with a list of battles and other actions in which they took part. With the Divisions it gives the Brigades and Battalions allocated to each for four or five intervals throughout the War. Allocation of Royal Artillery Brigades, ASC and other units is also given with many footnotes to explain deviations. [See also GHQ Staff Order of Battle (Note 6) which is not the same book nor does it give the same information.] See Figs. 6 and 7. A.F. Becke's book is a must for family historians wishing to trace their ancestor's war service. The reprinting of this series will make it far more available. The Imperial War Museum Printed Books Library has two sets, one with handwritten corrections. It is unfortunate that there is no index.

(35) *Soldiers Died in the Great War 1914—18.* (London, HMSO, 1921). In 80 paperbacked parts plus one for officers. Entries by Corps and Regiments, subdivided into Battalions; names then in alphabetical order. Gives Name, Number, where born, where enlisted (plus home town if different), when died and war zone. Does not give Corps unit but gives previous Battalion if transferred. All 80 volumes, plus the companion volume of *Officers Died in the Great War,* have now been reprinted and are obtainable from, among others, the Imperial War Museum at prices of between £10 and £35. ISBN 1871505 01 1 to 1 871505 80 1.

(36) *The National Roll of the Great War 1914—18.* This was published by the National Publishing Co., London. A total of 14 volumes appeared, the last in 1922. It is believed that the company then went into liquidation before the whole work could be completed. The method of obtaining the information is not known but some men whose names appear cannot recall being approached for details. Also a man who is known to have served in several units is listed as having only one posting. The 14 volumes are difficult to find, but there is a complete set in the Printed Books Library of the Imperial War Museum. Those marked * in the list following are in the Society of Genealogists' Library.

* Vol 1	London	* Vol 8	Leeds
* Vol 2	London	Vol 9	Bradford
* Vol 3	London	Vol 10	Portsmouth
Vol 4	Southampton	Vol 11	Manchester
* Vol 5	Luton	* Vol 12	Bedford and Northampton
Vol 6	Birmingham	* Vol 13	London
* Vol 7	London	Vol 14	Salford

The names are given in alphabetical order with the full home address. In some volumes the listing is divided into two or three parts. Each part must be searched and no hint is given that the volume is divided. Take care! Sometimes gives Battalion number; other times only Regiment. Maximum number of men mentioned is about 150,000–200,000, i.e. about 1 in 20 or 1 in 30. Some entries have been found to be inaccurate.

(37) *The War Graves of the British Empire.* Over 200 volumes, one for each cemetery. Subtitled *The Register of the Names of Those who Fell in the Great War and are Buried in the . . . . Cemetery.* Compiled and published by order of the Imperial War Graves Commission*, London, 1923. A copy of the appropriate volume is to be found in a bronze wall safe at each Cemetery. May be in some Reference Libraries. The Director General, The Commonwealth War Graves Commission, 2 Marlow Road, Maidenhead, Berks, SL6 7DX may be able to look up a name. Gives the following details: Name, Number, where born, where enlisted (plus home town if different), when died, next of kin. Gives Battalion but not Corps unit number. Also gives previous unit if transferred.

(38) *Soldiers Killed on the First Day of the Somme.* Ernest W. Bell. Lists 18,000 names with rank, regiment and number who died on 1st July 1916.

(39) *Badges and Insignia of British Armed Services.* Major W.Y. Carmen and Dr Tanner (Adam and Chas. Black, London).

(40) *Awards of Honour.* Capt. Arthur Jocelyn C.V.O. (Adam and Chas. Black, London).

(41) *Head Dress Badges of the British Army.* A.L. Kipling and H.L. King (Fred. Muller, London).

(42) *For Gallantry in the Performance of Military Duty.* A list of awards of the MSM for gallantry contains rank, number, name, unit, theatre of war and several citations. 64 pages.

(43) *The Medals, Decorations and Orders of the Great War 1914–1918.* A.A. Purves. 220 pages. 150 ribbons in full colour.

(44) Numerous books by J.M.A. Tamplin dealing with the recipients of various medals. These will assist you to identify units from photos and medals.

During the War several monthly or weekly illustrated magazines were

---

*The Imperial War Graves Commission became the Commonwealth War Graves Commission by Charter in 1964.

published. These are full of background detail and many pictures. Typical of these are:

(45) *The Great War. A Standard History of the All Europe Conflict.* Edited by H.W. Wilson and J.A. Hammerton. (Amalgamated Press, London.) 27 volumes.

(46) *The Times History of the Great War.* 20 volumes.

(47) *The War Budget.* Published weekly by the Daily Chronicle.

(48) *I Was There.* The human story of the Great War 1914–18. Editorial by Sir John Hammerton. (The Waverly Book Co. Ltd., London about 1938–40.) About 360 eyewitness accounts taken from named but undated printed sources. 4 volumes. Many photos, most from Imperial War Museum Photo Library, but unfortunately not numbered.

(49) *They Called it Passchendaele.* Lyn Macdonald. (Michael Joseph, London.) A collection of eyewitness accounts recorded in 1979–80 which was used as the basis of a BBC broadcast.

(50) *Roses of No-Mans-Land.* Lyn Macdonald. Stories by and about nurses. Also a BBC broadcast; and Channel 4 television documentary (1997).

(51) *Death's Men – Soldiers of the Great War.* Denis Winter. (Allen Lane.) Life in the trenches.

(52) *Men of Gallipoli.* Peter Liddle. (Allen Lane, London, 1976.) Has an extensive bibliography and a list of 600 men whose memoirs are available at the Brotherton Library (Leeds University) in the Liddle Archives.

(53) *Before Endeavours Fade.* Rose E.B. Coombs. (Battle of Britain Prints International Limited, London, 1976.) A guide to the Battle Fields as they exist today. Also gives a short history of the Imperial War Graves Commission.

Most Libraries have a selection of 'shipping' books around 387.24.

(54) *British Vessels Lost at Sea 1914–18.* A reprint of the official HMSO 1919 edition. (Patrick Stephens, 1977.) ISBN 0850592917. Beware! The page number sequence is in two sections each with a separate index. A large part of the book is taken up by a list of ships which were attacked but not sunk or even hit! Hence it includes a large proportion of troopship and transport fleets.

(55) *A Century of Cross Channel Passenger Ferries.* Ambrose Greenaway. (Ian Allen, 1981.)

(56) *Paddle Steamers 1837–1914.* Richard Clammer (B.T. Batford.)

The previous two items contain extensive bibliographies which should enable the researcher to find details of any ship.

The following four may also be of interest.

(57) *Cross Channel and Coastal Paddle Steamers.* F. Burtt. (R. Gilling, 1934.)

(58) *Irish Passenger Steamship Service.* 2 volumes. D.B. McNeill. (David and Charles, 1972.) Has a list of locations and photographs.

(59) *Railway and Other Steamers.* C.L.D. Duckworth. (T. Stephenson and Sons Limited, 1968.)

(60) *Hospital Ships and Ambulance Trains.* Lt.-Col. John H. Plumridge. (Seeley, Service and Co., London, 1975.) This gives a very full history of these two types of RAMC transport.

(61) A draft history of ASC units in Mesopotamia is given in WO161/17–19.

(62) *Royal Artillery Commemoration Book 1914–18.* Vols 1 and 2. (G. Bell and Son Limited, London.)

(63) There are three periodicals which cover the War and a look through back copies will reveal many additional books as well as articles on units and actions. (1) *Stand To!,* the journal of the Western Front Association. Three issues per year since 1980. Numbers 1–30 (Winter 1990). (2) *Bulletin* – the 'in-house' general news letter of the Western Front Association. Three issues per year since 1982. Numbers 1 to 49 (April 1997). Both these publications are available to members of the Western Front Association. Subscription £16.00 (June 1997). Membership Sec. Paul Hanson, 17 Aldrin Way, Cannon Park, Coventry CV4 7DP. There is also (3) *The Great War 1914–18* – the illustrated journal of the First World War History. Available from Broadsword Publishing, 6 Cranleigh Gardens, Sanderstead, South Croydon, Surrey CR2 9LD. £15.00 for four issues. About four issues per year. First published 1988.

Copies of these journals are available in the Imperial War Museum Printed Books Library.

(64) *Kitchener's Army. The Raising of the New Armies 1914–16.* Peter Simkins. (Manchester University Press, 1990) 0 7190 2638 5. Paperback.

(65) *British Battle Insignia. (1) 1914–18.* Mike Chappell. (Osprey Publishing, London, 1986.) ISBN 0 85045 727 0. No. 182 of the Osprey Men-at-Arms Series.

(66) Article *The Role and Composition of the Army Corps in the BEF.* Page 191 No. 22 Summer 1990 *Stand To!,* the journal of the Western Front Association.

20.3 NOTES

(1) The total number of men and women in the United Kingdom in uniform for at least some time during the War was about 5,060,000 or some 11% of the total population of 46,000,000. Of these, 47% or 2,377,876 became casualties. This number includes men who were wounded several times, so perhaps is a little on the high side. Deaths were 744,000 or nearly 9% of the male population aged between 25 and 40.

(2) Ministry of Defence, Army Search CS(R)2b, Bourne Avenue, Hayes, Middlesex, UB3 1RF.

(3) Medal rolls are now available at the PRO, Kew.

(4) **Army Definitions.**

Unit – This is taken to mean the defined body of men in which the ancestor served. It could be a Corps, Division, Brigade, Regiment, Battalion, Company, Battery, etc. The first four of these are so large that they are not precise enough to trace the ancestor or his activity, as these larger units were often split up and were posted to different areas.

Army – Either an undefined large body of fighting men, e.g. The British Army, or a defined unit of the British forces which was the largest sub-division of our forces and in 1914–18 had about 250,000 to 350,000 men. For example, the 4th Army.

Corps – A named Corps, such as the 'Army Service Corps' or the 'Tank Corps'; a large unit of up to 100,000 men who carried out their duties in small groups, often of only 100, called sections, Companies or Detachments, who were attached to the normal Army subdivisions in order to perform some specialised duty (doctors, engineers, etc.). To trace an ancestor's activities in a named Corps, the precise unit, etc. must be identified. Alternatively, an Army Corps (usually with a Roman number, e.g. XIII Corps) is the major subdivision of an Army. In 1914–18 an Army usually had three to six Corps, or more correctly Army Corps, each being itself subdivided into about four divisions (Ref. 66). However, the number of Divisions per Corps was not strictly adhered to and varied as circumstances changed. First World War Corps were numbered I to XXII and were allocated to the five Armies (four to an Army) but the allotment was changed frequently. This can lead to difficulty in tracing the ancestor's career. A close study of Ref. 34 would help.

Division – The major subdivision of a numbered (as opposed to a named) Corps. It was the smallest completely self-contained fighting unit in the army as it had in its normal establishment both the fighting troops and its own supporting troops, transport, artillery, etc. Total strength in 1914–18 was about 18,000 men, 4000 horses and 850 wagons. There were over 70 such Divisions which were numbered 1st, 2nd, etc. up to 71st plus three Cavalry Divisions (1st, 2nd and 3rd). A few Divisions also had names, e.g. 51st (Highland) Division.

Brigade – Either the sub-division of a Division, numbered from 1 to several hundred, e.g. 1st, 2nd Brigades. Each numbered Brigade was allocated to a numbered Division usually on a permanent basis at a rate of three Brigades per Division. A few Brigades were named, e.g. The Guards Brigade – made up of the Regiments of Foot Guards. A Brigade was sub-divided into four Battalions (reduced to three in 1918.) Alternatively, it could refer to a Brigade of artillery. Each Division had four Brigades attached to it, each Brigade having four Batteries of four guns. This meant that the total fire power was 64 guns although the number changed many times during the War. These Brigades were numbered in Roman numerals (as opposed to normal figures for Brigades of troops) and the numbering sequence ran through the whole of the other Forces, not just the Division to which they were attached. Numbers in the hundreds were common, e.g. CCXXIII. The Batteries within each

Brigade were numbered A, B, C, D for Horse and 1, 2, 3, 4, etc. for Field, Siege, Heavy and Mountain Artillery. During the War the Artillery arrangements were changed many times and the footnotes in Becke must be studied to find the movements of each Battery. In the later years of the War many of the heavier Batteries were attached to Corps or Armies, not to Divisions.

Battalion — A quarter of a Brigade; at the same time a sub-division of a Regiment. In peacetime a Regiment had two Battalions (1st and 2nd). During the War most regiments raised extra Battalions, sometimes up to 20 or more, and were thus scattered throughout several Divisions. Hence, you must know the ancestor's Battalion to trace his activities.

Regiment — A named body of men usually associated with a town or county, in peacetime about 2,000 men divided into 2 Battalions of 1,000 men. During the War, a town often raised many Battalions. In the First World War the term 'Regiment' was not a defined sub-division of an Army, but Battalions were given their Regimental battalion names, e.g. 12th East Surrey or 2nd/10th North London. It was almost as if the sole purpose of a Regiment was to act as a recruiting centre and a training 'factory' to supply Battalions to the Divisions.

Company — A sub-division of a Battalion. About 100–400 men or a unit of a named Corps working as a group, e.g. No. 24 Motor Ambulance Convoy (645 Coy ASC).

Platoon — A sub-division of a Company of about 30–50 men (Infantry).

Section — Part of an infantry platoon (10–15 men) or part of a Company of RE or ASC (50 men).

Army Troops, Corps Troops and Divisional Troops — Not, as it first appears, men who make up an Army, Corps or Division, but troops usually of an auxiliary (signals, transport, clerks, medical, etc.) nature reporting directly to and supporting the Headquarters of the Army, Corps or Division. They also include some special fighting troops, e.g. Heavy Artillery, Cavalry (Tanks) whose disposition is placed at the disposal of the HQ rather than the next lower echelon of command. Tended to be permanently attached to the HQ although the lower echelons were often changed. Often included was a company of soldiers for general 'odd jobs'.

GHQ Troops — The troops needed to run the GHQ plus some Corps units held as a general reserve.

Lines of Communication Troops — Troops under the direct control of GHQ, mainly connected with supply, etc. but not necessarily so, which provided a service for the whole of the British Forces in France.

Park — A place where ammunition, supplies and vehicles were stored together with the lorries which transported them. Also, the name of the type of unit

56

which manned the lorries, e.g. an Ammunition Supply Park was an ASC unit which arranged the transport and storage of ammunition for a Corps.

Field Ambulance — A unit (not just a vehicle) comprising both Army Service Corps and Royal Medical Corps men who manned a first aid post and drove motor and horse ambulances.

Convoy — A line of vehicles on the move and the unit which manned the vehicles and serviced them.

Regiment of Cavalry — About 500 men divided into three squadrons each of four Troops. The Troops of about 40 men were split into Sections. There were 28 Regiments of Cavalry — 7 Dragoon Guards and 21 Dragoons, Hussars and Lancers. There were also numerous regiments of Territorial Cavalry called Yeomanry — see Appendix l.

Cadre — or 'to reduce to a cadre'. If a unit suffered heavy losses or was to be reorganised it was often reduced to a few officers and men to keep the name on the books until it was re-formed with new men. With infantry battalions it usually meant a reduction to 10 officers and 45 other ranks (normal strength about 1,000 total), the surplus being sent to a Base depot for re-allocation although the Engineers, Artillery, etc. were often re-allocated within the immediate area.

(5) Allocations of Units.

These are lists issued from time to time to show which units of the various Corps were attached to which Divisions, Corps or Armies. These lists can often be found in the Corps Museum or at the PRO Kew.

ASC Allocations WO33/730/744/893.

Army Troop Allocations WO33/829/827.

Other Allocation Lists, including the ASC, RA and RAMC, can be found in WO95/5494. Part RAMC allocations can be found in Vol 3 of Ref. 29. Contents of WO95/5494:

Folder A — Allocation of Siege Batteries

Folder B — Allocation of Canadian Siege Batteries

Folder C — Allocation of Heavy Artillery Batteries

Folder D — Allocation of Royal Horse and Royal Field Artillery Batteries, two volumes

Folder E — Allocation of ASC units of all types with note of War Diary number

Folder F — Allocation of ASC units Motor Transport and Horse Transport only

Folder G — Allocation of ASC Motor Transport

Folder H — Index to RASC units

Folder I — Allocation of Machine Gun Companies

Folder J — Allocation of Entrenching Battalions

Folder K — Allocation of Medical Units

Folder L — Allocation of RAMC Locations

(6) Order of Battle of British Army in France General Staff GHQ.

Imperial War Museum Library. The PRO Kew has what is believed to be a complete set under the following Reference Numbers.

WO95/5467	France 1914—16
WO95/5468	France 1916—17
WO95/5469	France 1918—Dec 1918
WO95/5470	Rhine Army 1919

Other neighbouring sequences cover the Home Army and other War Zones. See also

WO33/911 Russia
WO33/795 Home Divisions } Possible duplicates of WO95/Series
WO33/829 Army Troops

(7) General Monthly Returns of the Regimental Strength of the British Army.

These have their own class at Kew — WO73/97—111 covers WWI. WO73/102 is Jan—April 1916. Each piece covers 4 months. WO33/763 and WO25/3548 also give lists of troop ship sailings to destinations other than France. Some of the lists in WO95/5494 give exact sailing dates of units.

(8) War Diaries.

Contained in WO95/... PRO Kew. If the unit cannot be found easily in the Class Index then WO95/5494 (Note 5) contains a miscellaneous collection of Allocation Lists for several Corps. These are notated with the War Diary piece number in several cases. Other notes index units of several Corps against the location in which they served and give the date of sailing. War Diaries of Home-based units are to be found in the index around WO95/5455.

(9) War Establishments.

Some are given in Miscellaneous War Office Papers in PRO Kew. WO33/743/778/900-902/789 and a complete set (?) in WO23/900— et seq. Others may be found in Regimental Museums.

(10) Prisoners of War.

There are no lists of prisoners of war in the PRO at Kew (PRO Leaflet No 72). Some may be mentioned in correspondence regarding prisoners in FO 383/... and CO 537/1123 (the latter covers British prisoners in Turkey). The International Red Cross in Geneva keeps lists of prisoners and internees for the War. They are housed in the International Red Cross Library in Geneva and there is currently no public access or enquiry service. (See The Central Tracing Agency of the International Committee of the Red Cross, C.R. Chapman, in *Family Tree Magazine,* Vol. 10, No. 7 (May), 1994.

(11) Visits to the Battle Field.

Read Rose Coombs' book (Ref. 53). Contact Galloway Travel Group of 31 Market

Hill, Sudbury, Suffolk CO10 6EN (Tel: 01787-76161), or Major and Mrs Holt's Battlefield Tours Ltd., Golden Key Building, 15 Market St., Sandwich, Kent CT13 9DA (Tel. 01304-612248), or The Tours Officers WFA, Lt.-Col. Graham Parker OBE, c/o No. 4 Spencer House, 45a Crystal Palace Road, East Dulwich, London SE22 9EX, all of whom arrange 'package tours to the battle areas'.

(12) Those who have one of the Plaques might be interested to know that the late Miss Rose E.B. Coombs of the Imperial War Museum has prepared an unpublished paper on the subject which gives a great deal of detail, including references to *The Times* concerning the competition (see page 9.)

(13) Leave.

The length of leave was increased from 10 to 14 days (both times including travel) on 1st November 1917. In December 1917 over 115,000 men in France had had no leave for over 12 months and some 5,000 none for 18 months. By January 1918, 5,500 officers and men were being sent on leave each day, itself quite a transport problem. Journey time from front line trench to front door was under 48 hours for most places in England and Wales.

(14) The British Red Cross has no records of soldiers or casualties but they do hold records of Red Cross and St John Ambulance personnel who served in Voluntary Aid Detachments in hospitals and homes, both in England and overseas. These include male and female ambulance drivers, some of whom later had to join the RAMC or ASC to comply with Army Regulations. Women drivers were supposed to be confined to the area of base hospitals but some at least strayed near enough to the front line to be awarded medals and to become casualties. Contact The Archivist, British Red Cross Training Centre, Barnett Hill, Wonersh, Guildford, Surrey GU5 3PJ. A list of Women Motor Drivers who were WAAC Drivers is in WO162/62 at the PRO Kew; gives number, name, initials, unit (in some cases only) and station; gives town for UK station or Overseas. WO95/3982 War Diaries of DDMS L of C gives lists of Nursing Sisters by name as they arrived in France.

(15) The Military Heraldry Society, Hon. Sec. Mr A. Grimston, 12 Glen Terrace, Clover Hill, Halifax HX1 2YN, takes an interest in unit emblems (see page 26, **NOT** Cap badges) and may be able to trace these patches. Their magazine *The Formation Sign* can be seen in the Imperial War Museum.

(16) The rearrangement of the Army in April 1915, which meant the disbanding and re-forming of a number of Divisions, is covered in great detail in the Appendix of Vol 3b of Becke (Ref. 34).

(17) Embarkation Dates.

WO162/7 is a manuscript list, the arrangement of which is difficult to understand. Use with care. It does include some of the more unusual units. The main embarkation series is WO25/3535 et seq.

(18) Michelin 1/200,000 maps (yellow and blue covers) are available from most good

booksellers. Stanfords of Long Acre, London also stock, or will order, the even more detailed and very expensive IGN series, both in the 1/50,000 and 1/25,000 scales (1¼ inches per mile and 2½ inches per mile). Copies of Michelin 1/200,000 sheets 51, 52, 54 (these are sub-sheets of sheet 236), albeit of an old edition, are available with an overprint showing all cemeteries. They can be obtained for a modest cost from the Commonwealth War Graves Commission, 2 Marlow Road, Maidenhead, Berks. SC6 7DX

(19) As a last hope, but only when much is already known, check the PRO Class Indexes for WO documents. WO32/..., WO 33/..., WO160/... and WO161/... are the most likely to reveal slender clues. Some draft unit histories are in CAB44/... and CAB45/...

(20) Those with ancestors in the Royal Artillery may find useful information in the private library of the Regiment at Woolwich. The staff are unable to carry out searches but could perhaps recommend suitable books. When the search has been narrowed, a visit could be arranged by appointment. Contact: The Historical Secretary, Royal Artillery Institution, Old Royal Military Academy, Woolwich, London SE18 4JJ.

(21) Researchers may also find useful contacts from The Western Front Association. See Ref. 63 for further details.

(22) Members of the Society of Friends (the Quakers) mostly refused to be called up or served in non-military posts such as the Friends Ambulance Unit. The Library at Friends House, Euston Road, London has returns from many of its 'Monthly Meetings', which very roughly equate to C of E Dioceses. There are about 60−70 returns listing Friends who were called up with details of how and where they served, if at all. There is no index. The Library also holds the published history of the Friends Ambulance Unit, which lists names, as well as several books on conscientious objectors.

APPENDIX I

A list of the Cavalry Regiments, Infantry Regiments and Corps of the British Army who served in the Great War 1914–18. The names given are those in use during that period.

CAVALRY

Household Cavalry

Life Guards – 1st and 2nd Regiments

Royal Horse Guards

Household Cavalry Composite Regiment. Formed from elements of the above three Battalions.

Household Battalion. Formed from elements of the Household Cavalry and fought as infantry.

Guards Divisional Cavalry Squadron. Formed from 1st Life Guards Reserve Regiment.

52nd (Siege) Battery RGA. Formed from Household Cavalry Personnel.

Dragoon Guards

1st King's Dragoon Guards

2nd Dragoon Guards (Queen's Bays)

3rd (Prince of Wales') Dragoon Guards

4th (Royal Irish) Dragoon Guards

5th (Princess Charlotte of Wales') Dragoon Guards

6th Regiment of Dragoon Guards (Carabiniers)

7th (The Princess Royal's) Dragoon Guards

Dragoons

1st (Royal) Dragoons

2nd Dragoons (Royal Scot Greys)

6th (Inniskilling) Dragoons

Hussars

3rd (King's Own) Hussars

4th (Queen's Own) Hussars

7th (Queen's Own) Hussars

8th (King's Royal Irish) Hussars

10th Prince of Wales' Own Royal Hussars

11th Prince Albert's Own Hussars

13th Hussars

14th (King's) Hussars

15th (King's) Hussars
18th (Queen Mary's Own) Hussars
19th (Queen Alexandra's Own Royal) Hussars
20th Hussars

Lancers

5th (Royal Irish) Lancers
9th (or Queen's Royal) Lancers
12th (Prince of Wales' Royal) Lancers
16th (The Queen's) Lancers
17th Lancers (Duke of Cambridge's Own)
21st (Empress of India's) Lancers

Cavalry Reserve

1st King Edward's Horse
2nd King Edward's Horse

Dragoons (Reserve)

4th Reserve Regiment Dragoons
Old 1st Reserve Cavalry Regiment (1st and 5th Dragoon Guards)
Old 2nd Reserve Cavalry Regiment (2nd Dragoon Guards and 6th Dragoons)
Old 3rd Reserve Cavalry Regiment (3rd and 6th Dragoon Guards)
Old 4th Reserve Cavalry Regiment (4th and 7th Dragoon Guards)
Old 5th Reserve Cavalry Regiment (1st and 2nd Dragoons)
6th Reserve Regiment of Dragoons

Lancers (Reserve)

1st Reserve Regiment of Lancers
Old 6th Reserve Cavalry Regiment (5th and 12th Lancers)
Old 7th Reserve Cavalry Regiment (9th and 21st Lancers)
Old 8th Reserve Cavalry Regiment (16th and 17th Lancers)

Hussars (Reserves)

2nd Reserve Regiment of Cavalry
3rd Reserve Regiment of Cavalry
5th Reserve Regiment of Cavalry
No 2 Cavalry Depot
No 3 Cavalry Depot
No 5 Cavalry Depot
North Irish Horse
South Irish Horse

Dragoons (Territorials)

2nd County of London
Shropshire Yeomanry

Queen's Own Yorkshire Dragoons
North Somerset Yeomanry
Duke of Lancaster's Own Yeomanry
Hampshire Yeomanry
Derbyshire Yeomanry
Hertfordshire Yeomanry
Berkshire Yeomanry
Montgomery Yeomanry
Lothian and Border Horse
Queen's Own Royal Glasgow Yeomanry
Fife and Forfar Yeomanry
Norfolk Yeomanry
Sussex Yeomanry
Glamorganshire Yeomanry
Essex Yeomanry
Northamptonshire Yeomanry
Lovat Scouts
Scottish Horse Yeomanry

Lancers (Territorials)

Lanarkshire Yeomanry
Surrey Yeomanry
Lincolnshire Yeomanry
Bedfordshire Yeomanry
East Riding of Yorkshire Yeomanry
City of London Yeomanry

Hussars (Territorials)

Ayrshire (Earl of Carrick's Own) Hussars Yeomanry
The Royal Buckinghamshire Hussars
The Denbighshire Hussars
The Cheshire Yeomanry (Earl of Chester's Hussars)
Royal 1st Devon Yeomanry (Hussars)
Royal North Devon Hussars Yeomanry
Dorset (Queen's Own) Yeomanry
Royal Gloucestershire Hussars, Yeomanry
Royal East Kent Yeomanry (The Duke of Connaught's Own Mounted Rifles)
Queen's Own West Kent Hussars
Lancashire Hussars
Leicestershire Yeomanry
1st County of London Yeomanry (Middlesex Duke of Cambridge's Hussars)
3rd County of London Yeomanry (Sharp shooters Hussars)
Northumberland Hussars

Nottinghamshire Yeomanry (Sherwood Rangers)
South Nottinghamshire Hussars
Queen's Own Oxfordshire Hussars
Pembroke Yeomanry
West Somerset Hussars
Staffordshire Yeomanry (Queen's Own Royal Regiment)
Suffolk Yeomanry (The Duke of York's Own Royal Suffolk Hussars)
Warwickshire Yeomanry
Westmorland and Cumberland Hussars
Royal Wiltshire Hussars (Prince of Wales' Own Royal Regiment)
Worcestershire Yeomanry (The Queen's Own Worcestershire Hussars)
Yorkshire Hussars (Alexandra, Princess of Wales' Own)
Imperial Camel Corps

Most of the Territorial units mentioned above, as well as some of the 6th Inniskilling Dragoons, served on foot, there being very little need for mounted troops in France after the battle of Mons in 1914. For this purpose pairs of Yeomanry Regiments were combined to form one battalion of infantry and renamed. Listed following are the Regiments involved and the battalions so formed.

Regiment of Cavalry	Infantry Battalion
1/1st Royal Devon Yeomanry 1/1st Royal North Devon Yeomanry	16th (Royal 1st Devon & R. Nth Devon Yeo.) Battn. Devonshire Regt.
1/1st West Somerset Yeomanry	12th (West Somerset Yeo.) Battn. Somerset L.I.
Regiment of Cavalry	Infantry Battalion
1/1st Fife and Forfar Yeomanry	14th (Fife and Forfar Yeo.) Battn. Royal Highlanders
1/1st Ayrshire Yeomanry 1/1st Lanark Yeomanry	12th (Ayr & Lanark Yeo.) Battn. Royal Scots Fusiliers
1/1st East Kent Yeomanry 1/1st West Kent Yeomanry	10th (Royal East Kent and West Kent Yeo.) Battn. East Kent Regiment
1/1st Sussex Yeomanry	16th (Sussex Yeo.) Battn. Royal Sussex Regiment
1/1st Suffolk Yeomanry	15th (Suffolk Yeo.) Battn. Suffolk Regiment
1/1st Norfolk Yeomanry	12th (Norfolk Yeo.) Battn. Norfolk Regiment.
1/1st Shropshire Yeomanry 1/1st Cheshire Yeomanry	10th (Shropshire & Cheshire Yeo.) Battn. Shropshire L.I.
1/1st Denbigh Yeomanry	24th (Denbigh Yeo.) Battn. Royal Welch Fusiliers

Regiment of Cavalry *(contd.)*	Infantry Battalion *(contd.)*
1/1st Montgomery Yeomanry	25th (Montgomery & Welsh Horse
1/1st Welsh Horse Yeomanry	Yeo.) Battn. Royal Welch Fusiliers
1/1st Pembroke Yeomanry	24th (Pembroke & Glamorgan Yeo.)
1/1st Glamorgan Yeomanry	Battn. Welsh Regiment
1/1st Lovat's Scouts Yeomanry	10th (Lovat's Scouts) Battn. The Q.O.
	Cameron Highlanders
1/1st Scottish Horse Yeomanry	13th (Scottish Horse Battn. The Black
	Watch) Royal Highlanders
2 Squadrons Glasgow Yeomanry	18th (Glasgow Yeo.) Battn. Highland
	Light Infantry
2 Squadrons Duke of Lancaster's	12th (Duke of Lancaster's Own Yeo.)
Own Yeomanry	Battn. Manchester Regt.
1/1 Yorkshire Hussars	9th (Yorkshire Hussars) Battn.
	West Yorkshire Regt.
2/1 Northumberland Hussars	9th (Northumberland Hussars) Battn.
	Northumberland Fusiliers
1/1 Lancashire Hussars	18th(Lancashire Hussars) Battn. The
	King's (Liverpool Regiment)
1 Squadron (Service) 6th	9th (North Irish Horse) Battn. Royal
Inniskilling Dragoons	Irish Fusiliers (Infantry Battalion)
'B' and 'C' Squadrons North	
Irish Horse (Regt. of Cavalry)	
1/1 Hampshire Yeomanry	15th (Hampshire Yeo.) Battn.
	Hampshire Regiment.
1/1 Westmorland and Cumberland	7th (Westmorland and Cumberland
Yeomanry	Yeomanry) Battn. Border Regiment
1/1 Royal Wiltshire Yeomanry	6th (Wiltshire Yeomanry) Battn.
	Wiltshire Regiment.
1st South Irish Horse	7th (South Irish Horse) Battn. Royal
2nd South Irish Horse	Irish Regiment.

ARTILLERY

Honourable Artillery Company
Royal Horse Artillery
Royal Field Artillery
Royal Garrison Artillery

INFANTRY

Foot Guards
Coldstream Guards
Scots Guards
Grenadier Guards
Irish Guards
Welsh Guards (formed 1915)
Guards Machine Gun Regiment

Infantry Regiments
The Queen's (Royal West Surrey Regiment)
The Buffs (East Kent Regiment)
The King's Own (Royal Lancaster Regiment)
The Northumberland Fusiliers
The Royal Warwickshire Regiment
The Royal Fusiliers (City of London Regiment)
The King's (Liverpool Regiment)
The Norfolk Regiment
The Lincolnshire Regiment
The Devonshire Regiment
The Suffolk Regiment
Prince Albert's (Somerset Light Infantry)
The Prince of Wales' Own (West Yorkshire Regiment)
The East Yorkshire Regiment
The Bedfordshire Regiment
The Leicestershire Regiment
The Royal Irish Regiment
Alexandra, Princess of Wales' Own (Yorkshire Regiment) = 'Green Howards'
The Lancashire Fusiliers
The Royal Scots Fusiliers
The Cheshire Regiment
The Royal Welch Fusiliers
The South Wales Borderers
The King's Own Scottish Borderers
The Cameronians (Scottish Rifles)
The Royal Inniskilling Fusiliers
The Gloucestershire Regiment
The Worcestershire Regiment
The East Lancashire Regiment
The East Surrey Regiment
The Duke of Cornwall's Light Infantry

The Duke of Wellington's (West Riding Regiment)
The Border Regiment
The Royal Sussex Regiment
The Hampshire Regiment
The South Staffordshire Regiment
The Dorsetshire Regiment
The Prince of Wales' Volunteers (South Lancashire Regiment)
The Welch Regiment
The Black Watch (Royal Highlanders)
The Oxfordshire and Buckinghamshire Light Infantry
The Essex Regiment
The Sherwood Foresters (Nottinghamshire and Derbyshire Regiment)
The Loyal North Lancashire Regiment
The Northamptonshire Regiment
Princess Charlotte of Wales' (Royal Berkshire Regiment)
The Queen's Own (Royal West Kent Regiment)
The Royal Scots (Lothian Regiment)
The King's Own (Yorkshire Light Infantry)
The King's (Shropshire Light Infantry)
The Duke of Cambridge's Own (Middlesex Regiment)
The King's Royal Rifle Corps = 'The Green Jackets'
The Duke of Edinburgh's (Wiltshire Regiment)
The Manchester Regiment
The Prince of Wales' (North Staffordshire Regiment)
The York and Lancaster Regiment
The Durham Light Infantry
The Highland Light Infantry
Seaforth Highlanders (Ross-shire, Buffs, The Duke of Albany's)
The Gordon Highlanders
The Queen's Own (Cameron Highlanders)
The Royal Irish Rifles
Princess Victoria's (Royal Irish Fusiliers)
The Connaught Rangers
Princess Louise's (Argyll and Sutherland Highlanders)
The Prince of Wales' Leinster Regiment (Royal Canadians)
The Royal Munster Fusiliers
The Royal Dublin Fusiliers
The Rifle Brigade (The Prince Consort's Own)
Channel Islands Militia
Honourable Artillery Company (Infantry)
The London Regiment

Inns of Court Officers Training Corps
The Monmouthshire Regiment
The Cambridgeshire Regiment
The Hertfordshire Regiment
The Herefordshire Regiment

CORPS

Corps of Royal Engineers
Army Cyclist Corps
The Northern Cyclist Battalion
The Highland Cyclist Battalion
The Kent Cyclist Battalion
The Huntingdonshire Cyclist Battalion
Royal Defence Corps
Army Service Corps
Royal Army Medical Corps
Labour Corps
Royal Army Ordnance Corps
Royal Army Veterinary Corps
Royal Army Pay Corps
Corps of Army Schoolmasters
Corps of Military Mounted Police
Corps of Military Foot Police
Corps of the Small Arms School
Military Provost Staff Corps
Non-Combatant Corps
Queen Mary's Army Auxiliary Corps
Machine Gun Corps
Tank Corps

The following units also existed and were mostly not Regiments but had separate badges:

Isle of Man Volunteers
Welsh Horse Yeomanry
First Aid Nursing Yeomanry
Queen Alexandra's Imperial Nursing Service
Chaplains Department
Army Service Corps Armoured Car Convoys
Army Remount Service
Army Scripture Readers
Forage Corps (for Women) formed 1916

Many Military Schools and Officers Training Corps

Royal Navy Regiment — later RN Division. Consisted of the following: Drake, Hawke, Benbow, Collingwood, Nelson, Howe, Hood, Anson, and the Machine Gun Battn.

Prisoner of War Companies

Military Prisons

A fuller list can be found in Ref. 33.

APPENDIX II

THE ARMY 1914-18

A List of Divisions

The Regular Army

The Guards Division
1st—8th Divisions and the 27th, 28th, 29th Divisions.

New Army Divisions

9th—26th and 30th—41st Divisions
43rd, 44th and 45th served only in India.
The 30th—35th Divisions were formed to found the 4th Army in the early days of the war. This army was disbanded and re-formed in April 1915. The composition of the Divisions was also changed at the same time.

Territorial Force Divisions

42nd—69th except 63rd Division.

Other Divisions

63rd Royal Navy
(Note: 70th Division was never formed.)
71st, 72nd, 73rd Home Service Divisions.
74th formed at El Arish from all British units of dismounted yeomanry.
75th formed at El Arish from some Indian units.

Cavalry Divisions

1st, 2nd and 3rd (4th and 5th were the old 1st and 2nd Indian Cavalry Divisions).

Other Mounted Divisions

1st, 2nd, 2nd/2nd, and 4th Mounted Divisions formed from Yeomanry. Mounted Yeomanry Division. Also 1st—5th Australian; 1st—4th Canadian; New Zealand; Portuguese 1st and 2nd.

Except where listed below, the above Divisions served only in France after sailing from England.

1st Mounted	} Served in	71st	} Served in
2nd/2nd Mounted	England only	72nd	England only
4th Mounted		73rd	
43rd	} Served in	64th	
44th	India only	65th	} Served in
45th		67th	England only
		68th	
		69th	

The following divisions spent some time in the countries named as well as France.

42nd
* 46th (sailed but recalled)
* 31st
* 11th
* 29th
52nd
53rd
54th (Not France)
2nd Mounted Division
* 63rd (Royal Naval)
* 10th (Not France)
* 13th (Not France)
74th
75th (Not France)
} Egypt 1914- June 1917 includes units in transit marked*

16th (Not France
22nd
26th
27th
28th
60th (Not France)
} Salonika (Greece) to June 1917

10th (Not France)
11th
29th
42nd
52nd
53rd
54th
27th
28th
Royal Naval (63rd)
13th (Not France)
2nd Mounted (dism/ted)
} Gallipoli Helles Sulva Mudros (on Lemnos)

13th Mesopotamia
45th Mesopotamia (part)

52nd
54th (Not France)
74th
75th (Not France)
53rd (Not France)
60th (Not France)
10th (Not France)
many assorted mounted units
} Palestine June 1917– 1918

48th
41st
23rd
7th
5th
} Italy

22nd
26th
27th
28th
} Macedonia Greece Bulgaria.

10th Div. Russia — not France

59th Ireland

In addition to the usual numbers some divisions were given names. These should not be confused with Battalion names, although the method of indicating Territorial Divisions was similar to that used for Territorial Battalions.

1/ = 1st Line Territorial Unit
2/ = 2nd Line Territorial Unit
3/ = 3rd Line Territorial Unit

9th Div. Scottish
11th Div. Northern
12th Div. Eastern
15th Div. Scottish
16th Div. Irish
17th Div. Northern
18th Div. Eastern
19th Div. Western
20th Div. Light
30th Div. Ulster
38th Div. Welsh
42nd Div. 1st East Lancashire
46th Div. 1st North Midland
47th Div. 1/2nd London

48th Div. 1/1st South Midland
49th Div. 1/1st West Riding
50th Div. 1/1st Northumbrian
51st Div. Highland
55th Div. 1/1st West Lancashire
56th Div. 1/1st London
57th Div. 2nd West Ham
58th Div. 2/1st London
59th Div. 2nd North Midland
60th Div. 2/2nd London
61st Div. 2nd South Midland
62nd Div. 2nd West Riding
63rd Div. Royal Naval
66th Div. 2nd East Lancashire

APPENDIX III

THE BRITISH FORCES IN FRANCE
1916

Besides infantry, the British Army had many other types of unit. A list of some of the various types for July 1916 is given below. By the end of the War a few others had been added and in some cases command or allocation of units had been transferred. The list is by no means complete but it gives an idea of the variety of units. The numbers in the left-hand column give a rough idea of the total number of units of that type in France.

Units directly under GHQ

These were often allocated to one of the four (later five) Armies but they reported to GHQ There were also Lines of Communication Troops which served all five Armies.

Total No. of Units in France	Type of Unit	Name of Corps
	GHQ Wireless Signal Company	RE
22	Searchlight Sections	RA
91	Sound Ranging Companies	RA
	Anti Aircraft Artillery	RA
5	Special Battalion	RE (Gas)
	Special Works Park	RE (Camouflage)
	Wireless Depot	RE
	Wireless School	RE
42	Ordnance Companies	ROC
	Base Camouflage Works	RE
	GHQ Troop Company	RE
	Army Post Office	RE and later APS
	Base Stationery Depot	RE
	Publications Department	RE
	Army Printing Depot	RE
	Printing and Photography Company	RE
	Rubber Stamp Factory	RE
	Typewriter Repair Service	RE
5	Supply Depots	ROC
41	Ambulance Trains (2 types)	RAMC

Units directly under GHQ *(contd.)*

Total No. of Units in France	Type of Unit	Name of Corps
80	Hospitals (several types)	RAMC
26	Mobile Labs (4 types)	RAMC
16	Convalescent Homes	RAMC
5	Supply Depots (medical)	RAMC
19	Supply Depots	ASC
45	Field Bakeries	ASC
58	Bakery Sections	ASC
29	Field Butchers	ASC
10	Remount Depot (horse replacements)	ASC
1	Training School	ASC
5	Ambulance Flotilla (barges)	RAMC and RE
	War Dog Training School	RE
24	Veterinary Hospitals	AVC
18	Veterinary Evacuating Sec.	AVC
2	Veterinary Stores	AVC
1	Veterinary Laboratory	AVC
1	Veterinary Disposal Branch	AVC
	Ordnance Base Work Shop	ROC
	Messenger Dog Section	RE
12	Infantry Labour Battalions	Formed from Infantry Regts.
11	Labour Corps Companies	LC
8	Non-combatant Companies	
30	Labour Companies	ASC
3	Labour Companies Naval	
2	Railway Companies	ASC
73	Railway Supply Detachments	ASC
5	Auxiliary (Petrol) Companies	ASC
	Auxiliary (Bus) Company	ASC
	Auxiliary (Steam) Company	ASC
	Auxiliary (Water) Company	ASC
84	Depot Units of Supply	ASC
	Advance Park Company	RE
	Base Park Company	RE
4	Field Survey Companies	RE
4	Artisan Work Companies	RE
38	Lines of Communication Supply Companies	ASC

Army Troops

Units under the control of an Army were termed Army Troops and could consist of the following.

Total No. of Units in France	Type of Unit	Name of Corps	Total per Army
	Special (Projector) Companies (Gas)	RE	3
	Special (Mortar) Companies	RE	1
	Advanced Parks	RE	2
51	Army Troops Companies	RE	16
6	Siege Companies	RE	2
25	Tunnelling Companies	RE	8
	Electrical & Mechanical Company	RE	1
	Boring Section	RE	1
	Army Workshop	RE	1
	Sound Ranging Sections	RE	7
	Observation Groups	RE	7
	Anti-Aircraft Searchlight Sections	RE	6
	Foreway Company (in charge of tramways etc. in defended zones)	RE	1
	Airline Sections	RE	3
	Cable Sections	RE	2
	Light Railway Signal Section	RE	1
	Signal Construction Section	RE	1
	Tunnelling School	RE	1
	Mining Companies	RE	1
	Mine Rescue School	RE	1
	Field Survey Company	RE	1
	Artisan Work Company	RE	1
	Motor Mobile Lofts for pigeons	4	
	Horse Drawn Mobile Lofts for pigeons	12	
	Fixed Loft for pigeons	1	
	Garrison Guard Conpany	1	
	Military Police Traffic Control		squadron 1, company 1
	Auxiliary Companies	ASC	3
	Pontoon Parks, M.T. Companies	ASC	2
	Army Troops, M.T. Companies	ASC	3

Army Troops *(contd.)*

Total No. of Units in France	Type of Unit	Name of Corps	Total per Army
	Mobile Repair Unit	ASC	1
	Siege Battery Transport	ASC	2
	Water Tank Company	ASC	1
31	Motor Ambulance Convoys	ASC and RAMC	5
60	Casualty Clearing Stations	RAMC	10
18	Advanced Depots Medical Stores	RAMC	2
25	Mobile Laboratories	RAMC	5
5	Mobile Dental Units	RAMC	1
	Stationary Hospital	RAMC	1
	Sanitary Sections	RAMC	15
5	X-Ray Units	RAMC	1
	Heavy Mobile Workshop	ROC	1
	Light Mobile Workshops	ROC	2
	Ordnance Gun Park	ROC	1
	Officers' Clothing Depot	ROC	1
	Forestry Companies	RE	3
	Labour Companies (British)		60
	Area Employment Companies		8
	Area Employment (Garrison Guard) Companies		5
	Italian Labour Companies		34
	Prisoner of War Companies		25
	Indian Labour Companies		11
	Chinese Labour Companies		10
	Army Printing & Stationery Services Section		1
	RHA Army Section	RA	1
	RFA Army Brigade	RA	23
	RGA Army Brigade	RA	22
	RGA Siege Batteries	RA	15
	AA Batteries	RA	4
	AA Workshop	ASC	1
	Cavalry Divisions		1
	Barge Filtration Unit	RE	1
	Advanced Photographic Section	RE	1

Similarly, **Corps Troops** could consist of

	Name of Corps	Units per Corps
A regiment of cavalry		1
Cyclist Battalion		1
Motor Machine Gun Battery	MGC	1
Corps Signal Company	RE	1
ASC Heavy Artillery (Transport) Company	ASC	1
Supply Columns (1 for each Division)	ASC	4 or 5
Mobile Ordnance Workshops	ROC	2
Corps Ammunition Park	ASC	1
Heavy Artillery Groups	RA	2
Army Troop Companies	RE	2
Tunnelling Company	RE	
Royal Flying Corps	RFC	
Special Works Park (Camouflage)	RE	1
Field Cashier	APC	
Ordnance Officer and Staff		
Postal Service Detachment		
Army Chaplains Department		
Veterinary Units		
Plus any Army Troops allocated to the Corps.		

Likewise, **Divisional Troops**

	Name of Corps	Units per Division
Cavalry Squadron		1
Cyclist Company		1
Batteries Artillery	RA	16 (64 Guns)
Trench Mortar Batteries	RA	3
Field Company Engineers	RE	3
Signal Company	RE	1
Pioneer Battalion		1
Company of Divisional Train (Horse)	ASC	4
Field Ambulances	RAMC	3
Sanitary Section	RE	1
Mobile Veterinary Section	AVC	1
Infantry Labour Battalion		1

Divisional Troops *(contd.)*

	Name of Corps	Units per Division
Field Ambulance Workshop (up to April 1916)	ASC	1
Ordnance Officers		5
Chaplains		17
Post services	APS	1
Machine Gun Company (formed April 1917)	MGC	1
Plus any Corps Troop units allocated to the Division.		

The complement of all ranks in a Division varied during the War but was around 18,000. Similarly, the number of guns varied in size and number. A typical breakdown of numbers would be

infantry   12,000
artillery   4,000
others   2,000.

Within a Battalion, of which there were 12 per Division (reduced to 9 in January 1918), there would be

1 Signal Section — part of the RE Company
Cooks
Sanitary Section
Stretcher Bearers
Transport Drivers   Total about 200 supplied by
    mostly handcarts   Battalion from its own men
    and wagons
Bandsmen

RAMC officer in Regimental Aid Post.
A Battalion would have about 32 officers and 992 other ranks.

Army Service Corps

The total number of

ASC Motor Transport Companies	605
ASC Horse Transport Companies	552
ASC Mobile Repair Depots	22
ASC Mobile Depots	21

Royal Engineers

The Royal Engineers had 77 different types of unit (many shown above). The total of all RE units was 531.

APPENDIX IV

A List of the Battles involving British Troops
in France and Belgium

A more expansive list can be found in A.F. Becke's *Order of Battle Divisions.* A list of actions which took place during the period covered by each volume is given in *The Official History* series. The battles have names defined by the Historical Section of the Committee of Imperial Defence London and printed in their book *Principal Events 1914–18,* HMSO. A copy is to be found in WO161/102 and a second copy with annotations of participating units is in WO161 /103. This was reprinted by the London Stamp Exchange, 1988.

1914

23rd August	**Battle of Mons**
1st September	Fighting at Compiegne.
6th–9th September	**Battle of the Marne**
14th–28th September	**Battle of the Aisne**
18th September–16th October	Battle of Flanders
13th October–2nd November	Battle of Armentiers
13th October	Capture of Meteren
12th October–17th November	**1st Battle of Ypres**
18th–23rd December	Battle of Givenchy

1915

23rd February	Capture of Trench at Givenchy
10th–12th March	**Battle of Neuve-Chapelle**
17th April	Capture of Hill 60
22nd April–14th May	2nd Battle of Ypres
15th–25th May	Battle of Festubert
3rd June	Gain at Givenchy
9th August	Capture of Trench near Hooge
25th September–5th October	**Battle of Loos and Champagne**
25th September	Bois Grenier

1916

27th March–16th April	Fighting at St Eloi
21st May	German Attack on Vimy Ridge
1st July–18th November	**Battles of the Somme**

1916 *(contd.)*

During this period many actions were fought. They included

1st–13th July	Battle of Albert
2nd–4th July	Capture of la Boiselle
10th July	Capture of Contalmaison
14th–17th July	Battle of Bazentin Ridge
15th July–3rd September	Battle of Delville Wood
20th–25th July	Attack on High Wood
23rd July–3rd September	Battle of Pozieres Ridge
3rd–6th September	Battle of Guillemont
9th September	Battle of Ginchy
2nd–22nd September	Battle of Flers-Courcelette
15th September	Capture of Martinpuich
26th–28th September	Battle of Thiepval
25th–28th September	Battle of Morval
1st–18th October	Battle of Transloy Ridges
1st–3rd October	Capture of Eaucourt l'abbaye
7th October	Capture of Le Sars
7th October–5th November	Attacks on Butte de Warlencourt
3rd–11th November	Battle of the Ancre Heights
13th–18th November	Battle of the Ancre

1917

7th January	Raid south of Armentiers
23rd January	Raid at Neuville
29th January	Raid at Butte de Warlencourt
7th February	Capture of Grandecourt
23rd February–5th April	**German Retreat to the Hindenburg Line**
23rd February	Fighting near Gueudecourt
24th February	Capture of Petit Miraumont
26th February	Capture of Le Barque
28th February	Capture of Gommecourt
10th March	Capture of Irles
17th March	Capture of Bapaume
18th March	Capture of Peronne
9th April–3rd May	**Battle of Arras**
9th–14th April	1st Battle of the Scarpe
9th–14th April	**Battle of Vimy Ridge**
23rd–24th April	2nd Battle of the Scarpe
28th–29th April	Battle of Arleux
3rd–4th May	3rd Battle of the Scarpe

16th April–9th May	2nd Battle of the Aisne (mostly French)
13th–16th May	Capture of Roeux
7th–14th June	**Battle of Messines**
1st July	Attack on Lievin
15th–25th August	Battle of Hill 70, Lens
31st July–10th November	**Battle of Ypres (3rd Ypres)**
31st July–2nd August	Battle of Pilckem Ridge
16th–18th August	Battle of Lanemarck
19th August	The Cockcroft
22nd August	Fighting in front of St Julien
22nd–25th September	Battle of Menin Road Bridge
26th–30th September	Battle of Polygon Wood
4th October	Battle of Broodseinde
9th October	Battle of Poelcappelle
12th October	1st Battle of Passchendaele
26th October–2nd November	2nd Battle of Passchendaele
20th November–3rd December	**Battle of Cambrai**
20th–21st November	The Tank Attack
21st November	Recapture of Noyelles
23rd–28th November	Capture of Bourlon Wood
30th November–3rd December	The German Counter Attacks
30th November	Attack on Gouzeaucourt
1st December	Attack on Villers Guislain and Gauche Wood
30th December	Welch Ridge

1918

21st March–4th April	**1st Battle of the Somme**
21st–23rd March	Battle of St Quentin
24th–25th March	Action of the Somme Crossing
24th–25th March	1st Battle of Bapaume
28th March	1st Battle of Arras
26th–27th March	Battle of Rosieres
5th April	Battle of the Avre
28th June	La Becque
9th–29th April	**Battles of the Lys**
9th–11th April	Battles of Estaires
12th–15th April	Battles of Hazebrouck
13th–15th April	Defence of Hinges Ridge
13th–15th April	Battle of Bailleul
9th–17th April	1st Defence of Givenchy
17th–19th April	1st Battle of Kemmel Ridge

1918 *(contd.)*

18th April	Battle of Bethune
12th–15th April	Defence of the Nieppe Forest
18th–19th April	2nd Defence of Givenchy
25th–26th April	2nd Battle of Kemmel Ridge
29th April	Battle of Scherpenberg
20th–31st July	**Battles of the Marne**
20th–31st July	Battle of Tardenois
20th–31st July	Fighting in the Andre Valley
24th August–3rd September	**2nd Battle of the Somme**
21st–23rd August	Battle of Albert
24th August	Capture of Mory Copse
25th August	Capture of Belagnies and Sapignies
31st August–3rd September	2nd Battle of Bapaume
5th August–18th September	**The Advance in Flanders**
5th–11th August	Battle of Amiens
18th August	Capture of Outtersteene Ridge
18th August	Capture of Hoegennacker Ridge
24th August	Capture of Givenchy Craters
1st September	Capture of Neuve Eglise
2nd September	Capture of Wulverghem
4th September	Capture of Ploegsteert and Hill 63
17th September	Capture of Canteleux Trench
26th August–3rd September	**2nd Battle of Arras**
26th–30th August	Battle of the Scarpe
3rd September	Assault of the Drocourt-Queant Line
18th September–9th October	**Battles of the Hindenburg Line**
12th September	Battle of Havrincourt
18th September	Battle of Epehy
21st September	The Knoll
24th September	Attack on Quadrilateral and Fresnoy
27th September	Battle of the Canal du Nord
29th September	Passage at Bellenglise
29th September–1st October	Battle of the St Quentin Canal
1st October	Capture of Mont sur l'Oeuvre
3rd–5th October	Battle of Beaurevoir Line
8th–9th October	Battle of Cambrai
8th October	Capture of Forenville
8th October	Capture of Niergnies
9th October	Capture of Cambrai

The Final Advance

1918

17th October—11th November in Picardy

20th October	Capture of Solesmes
23rd October	Capture of Grand Champ Ridge
23rd October	Capture of Bousies
17th—25th October	Battle of the Selle
23rd October	Attack on Forest and Ovillers
1st & 2nd November	Battle of Valenciennes
1st November	Capture of Mont Houy
2nd November	Attack S.W. of Landrecies
4th November	Battle of the Sambre
	Capture of Le Quesnoy
5th—7th November	Passage of the Grand Honnelle
9th November	Occupation of Maubeuge

2nd October—11th November in Artois

7th—8th October	Forcing the Rouvroy-Fresne Line
17th October	Capture of Douai
17th October	Occupation of Lille
11th November	Capture of Mons

28th September—11th November in Flanders

28th September—2nd November	Battle of Ypres
14th—19th October	Battle of Courtrai
25th October	Ooteghem
31st October	Tieghem

SOME ACTIONS OUTSIDE FRANCE*

8th August 1914—1st December 1917	British in German East Africa
20th August 1914—18th February 1916	British in Cameroons
19th September 1914—9th July 1915	British in German S.W. Africa
3rd—21st November 1914	British in Suez and Akaba
11th—17th November 1914	Mesopotamia
1st January 1915—31st December 1917	British in British East Africa
19th February—19th March 1915	British attack Dardanelles
17th April—28th September 1915	Tigris — Kut al Amara
23rd April 1915—9th January 1916	British in Gallipoli
8th August 1915	Anzacs at Sulva Bay
5th October 1915—November 1918	British in Salonika
11th—22nd November 1915	River Euphrates

---

*The dates given refer to battles or periods of action and not to the length of time that British troops remained in the area.

25th November 1915–29th April 1916	British under siege in Kut
5th–12th August 1916	British advance into Sinai
13th December 1916–3rd April 1917	Fighting in Kut and Baghdad
1st January 1917–20th March 1917	British advance into Palestine
21st July–28th September 1917	British Forces at River Euphrates
7th October–7th November 1917	Battle of Gaza
5th November–9th December 1917	British capture Jerusalem
7th November 1917–1st March 1918	British Forces in Italy
3rd December 1917–23rd October 1918	British in Mesopotamia
1st January–30th September 1918	British advance along River Jordan
3rd April–31st December 1918	British Forces in Russia

FACTS

1. Howard White HOLDING, M2/153147 Private ASC (taken from medal still in family).
2. Awarded British War Medal and Victory Medal — Medal Office.
3. Was at one time Lance Corporal — photo with stripe. Fig.10.
4. Wears on lower left arm single inverted stripe (photo).
5. Wears on lower right arm small inverted triple stripe (photo).
6. Earliest known Army service — 25th February 1916(Postcard — UK Postmark) Fig.9.
7. Earliest known Army service in France — 18th June 1916(Card from France). Fig.11.
8. Latest known Army service — in Brussels — (27th April)? 1919. Postcard with Belgian postmark. (Almost unreadable.)
9. Only known locations

   NAMUR — 12th February 1919 (photo), Fig.12.

   WATERLOO — en route to Brussels 27th April ? 1919(Postcard).

These may have been taken during 'educational visits' after the 1918 Armistice prior to demob and hence not true postings.

10. Two group photographs.

    (a) Taken in England while under training and before 25th February 1916, showing 10 men (including a Sergeant) in a workshop. (Postcard as 6.)

    (b) Taken outside a German Horse Hospital on 12th February 1919 in NAMUR showing 13 men. Besides my father, one other (possibly 2) men appear in both photos. (Same photo as 9.) Fig.12.

11. He was a trained apprenticed Railway Engine Fitter and just prior to call-up a Lorry Design Draughtsman and he may have worked on the buses as a fitter.

UNSUBSTANTIATED FACTS AND TRADITIONS

12. He was a Vehicle Fitter in the Army (remembered as being on lost discharge papers).
13. He worked on ambulances — vague memories of relatives.
14. He was stationed near Albert at Christmas 1916 or 1917 (picture postcard sent at Christmas shows view of Albert).
15. He served only in Northern Europe — vague memory.
16. He was twice mentioned in despatches (remembered as being on lost discharge papers).
17. He was once in Amiens (remembered inscription in French Bible — now lost).
18. He was to go to Germany in the Army of Occupation but in the end did not go. (Comment from his girlfriend who was glad that he did not go.)

Fig. 1. Information relating to Private Howard White Holding.

ASSUMPTIONS FROM FIG. 1

A. He served in a motor transport workshop with the ASC (Facts 1, 10, 11, 12).
B. As he was with a workshop, the unit would remain intact throughout the war except for traceable transfers and amalgamations. (Far behind the line and therefore few casualties.) Dangerous assumptions but no alternative with the limited data available.
C. He went overseas between 28th Feb. (Fact 6 says *on leave until noon 28th Feb.*) and 18th June 1916 (Fact 7). As leave was most likely to be embarkation leave, date of sailing is at the beginning of March rather than at any other time.
D. He was at Namur on 12th Feb. 1919 (Facts 9 and 10). The men look too untidy to be far from the camp.
E. He may have been near Albert at Christmas 1916 or 1917 (Fact 14).
F. He may have worked on ambulances (Fact 13).

DEDUCTIONS FROM FIG.1

i. About 60 ASC Motor Transport Units left England between the two dates. (From Monthly Returns, War Diaries and Allocation Lists in WO95/5494.)
ii. About 76 ASC Motor Transport Units could have been in Namur area in Feb. 1919. (GHQ Order of Battle, War Diaries, Becke.)
iii. Only six units are in both lists — only two of these had ambulances — both MACs. An MAC Workshop had only 12 men (see Fact 10).
iv. No. 24 MAC did not go near Albert.
v. No. 21 MAC was within 3½ miles of Albert at Christmas 1916.
vi. Assume No. 21 MAC is ancestor's unit.
vii. Both No. 21 and No. 24 MACs left UK in early March 1916.
viii. Proof: ancestor's name is in the War Diary of No. 21 MAC (an extra and unexpected bonus).

Fig. 2. Information obtained from Fig. 1.

Fig. 3. Views of army camps in the UK can be found at postcard fairs, flea markets and car boot sales. The picture shows a typical card depicting the ancestor's camp.

41st DIVISION

TOTAL DIVISIONAL STRENGTH - 18,000 MEN

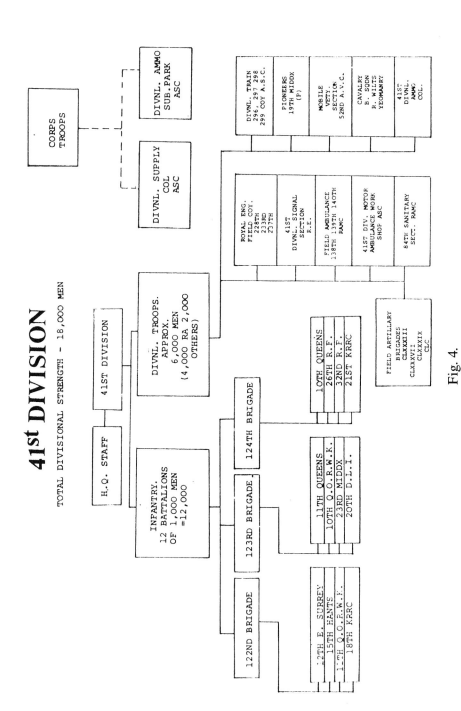

Fig. 4.

ARMY ORGANISATION

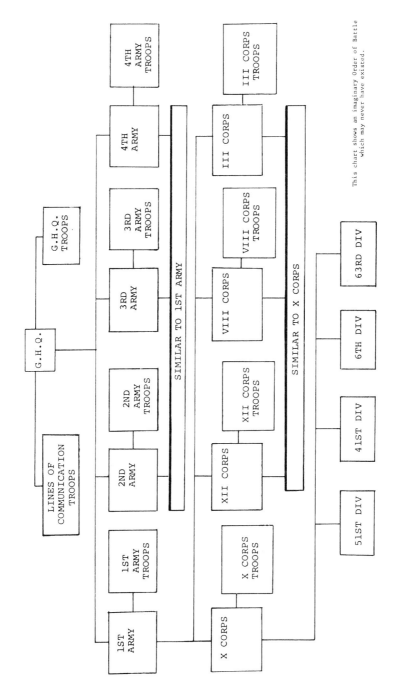

Fig. 5.

This chart shows an imaginary Order of Battle which may never have existed.

EXTRACT OF THE ENTRY FOR THE 41ST DIVISION IN BECKE'S ORDER OF BATTLE

Showing the type of information given in the tables and footnotes as at April 1916 at which time the Division was in England. The book repeats the information with appropriate footnotes at approximately 6 monthly intervals.

Brigades	Battalions	Mounted Troops	Field Artillery Brigades	Batteries
122 [2,3]	12/E. Surr.,15/Hants., 11/QORWK,18/KRRC [3]	B. Sqdn. R Wilts Yeo. [6,14]	CLXXXIII(H) [8]	A(H) B(H) C(H) [16] D(H)
123 [2,4]	11/Queens, 10/QORWK [4], 23/Middx., 20/DLI		CLXXXVII	A B C D [17]
124 [2,5]	10/Queens, 26R.F., 32/R.F., 21KRCC	41st Div. Cyclist Coy [7,15]	CLXXXIX	A B C D [18]
			CXC	A B C D [19]

Brigades	Brigade Amm. Colns.	Divisional Amm.Coln.	Field Coy-Engineers	Divisional Signal Section	Pioneers
122	CLXXXIII (H) BAC		228th [9]		
123	CLXXXVII BAC	41st D.A.C. [8]	233rd [9]	41st [9]	19/Middx [10] (P)
124	CLXXXIX BAC, CXC BAC		234th [9]		

Brigades	Field Ambulances	Mobile Vety.Sect.	Divnl. Train
122	138 [11]		
123	139 [11]	52nd [12]	41st [13]
124	140 [11]		

Fig. 6.

1. Formed at Aldershot in September 1915 as 41st Div. This Division was a new formation.
2. The Inf. Bdes. raised in 1915 as the 122nd, 123rd and 124th Bdes. were new formations.
3. The Bns. were designated Bermondsey, 2nd Portsmouth, Lewisham, and Arts and Crafts. On 16.10.15, 11/Q.O.R.W.K. joined 122nd Bde. from 118th Bde., 39th Div.
4. The Bns. were designated Lambeth, Kent County, 2nd Football, and Wearside. On 16.10.15, 10/Q.O.R.W.K. joined 123rd Bde. from 118th Bde., 39th Div.
5. The Bns. were designated Battersea, Bankers, East Ham, and Yeomen Rifles.
6. Sqdn. joined Div. before 20.11.15 at Aldershot. The Sqdn. disembarked at Le Havre on 6.5.16.
7. Coy. was formed in the Div. before 20.11.15 at Aldershot. The Coy. disembarked at Le Havre on 6.5.16.
8. The Artillery Bdes. were designated Hampstead, Fulham, Hackney, and Wimbledon. The D.A.C. was designated West Ham. The Bdes. were raised as 4-battery brigades; in each brigade the batteries were lettered A, B, C, and D, and each battery was a 4-gun battery. The Divnl. Arty. disembarked at Le Havre between 2—5.5.16.
9. The 3 Fd. Cos. were designated Barnsley, Ripon, and Reading; the Coy. was designated Glasgow. The companies disembarked at Le Havre between 2.5.16 and 6.5.16.
10. The Pioneer Bn. was designated 2nd Public Works and it joined the Div. at Aldershot before 20.11.15. The Bd. disembarked at Le Havre on 2.5.16.
11. The 3 Fd. Ambces. were trained at Crookham; they went to France with the Div. and disembarked at Le Havre between 3.5.16 and 6.5.16.
12. The Sec. joined the Div. at Aldershot before 20.11.15; it disembarked at Le Havre on 5.5.16.
13. The Train consisted of 296, 297, 298, and 299 Cos. A.S.C. It at Mytchett, went to France with the Div., and disembarked at Le Havre between 2.5.16 and 5.5.16.
14. Sqdn. left the Div. on 31.5.16, was attached to 2nd. Cav. Div. from 1.6.16 to 21.6.16 and joined IX Corps Cav. Regt. on 22.6.16.
15. Coy. left the Div. on 28.5.16 and joined II Corps Cyclist Bn. that day.
16. On 27.5.16, A(H), B(H), and C(H) left CLXXXIII and became D(H)/CLXXXIX, D(H)/CLXXXVII, and D(H)/CXC; and D/CLXXXVII, and D/CXC joined and became A, B, and C/CLXXXIII; D(H) remained D(H)/CLXXXIII.
17. On 27.5.16, D left and became B/CLXXXIII; and B(H)/CLXXXIII joined and became D(H)/CLXXXVII.
18. On 27.5.16, D left and became A/CLXXXIII; and A(H)/CLXXXIII joined and became D(H)/CLXXXIX.
19. On 27.5.16, D left and became C/CLXXXIII; and C(H)/CLXXXIII joined and became D(H)/CXC.

Fig. 7. Notes on Fig. 6.

Instructions regarding War Diaries and Intelligence Summaries are contained in F.S. Regs. Part II. and the Staff Manual respectively. Title pages will be prepared in manuscript.

WAR DIARY
— INTELLIGENCE SUMMARY.
(Erase heading not required)

21st Motor Ambulance Army [?]
Convoy.
April 1919.

Place	Date	Hour	Summary of Events and Information	Remarks and references to Appendices
NAMUR.	9/4/19	–	No. Orderly Officer - Sitting 1. O.Rs. Playing 12. The y/m N.C.O. drew and struck off the strength for to-day, having been despatched to Aust. Corps Cav. Camp for demobilization — M2/15347 L/Cpl. Holling. H.W., DM2/118524 Pte. Blackford. R. #M2/073698 Pte. Pattison. W.N., 43005 Pte. Cadman. J. Pte. March. b. was transferred with Dennis Fire Engine lorry to 4th Area Troops M.T. Coy. No. 67475 Pte. A/U/P. Sgt. Jones was promoted A/Cpl. with pay fm 3.4.19. No. 154164. Pte. Doheen. E.S. was declared fm 48 Clt. to day. Capt. P.T. Jones was admitted to 47 C.C.S. to day. The Convoy moved to BEEZ to day.	
BEEZ	10/4/19	–	Cars barged through. Limber 3. Nil. No. Orderly Officer lying 5. Sitting 3. O.Rs. lying 54. Sitting 22. Evacuation fm 47 and 48 C.C.S. — 0.Rs. lying 3. Sitting 5.	
	11/4/19	–	Cars barged through. Limbers 2. No. Orderly officers. M.I. O.R. Sitting 5. During the night of 10-11 2 wheels complete india rubber and 2 Warland Rims complete were withdrawn from the cars from the park. No. 58208 Pte. Sgt. G.A. 749 A.E.Cy. was awarded 7 days C.B. on the following charge "Absent from B.O.A.M. parade until he found in bed at 9.30 AM. Cars barged through. Limbers 4.	

'Same old place   Postmark
Friday night'   'S.E.
                                                    7.30pm
                                                    25 Feb 16'

Dear Mabel,
    Just a line to let you know I am going home on pass from tonight until Monday at Noon.
What do you think of the Workshop lads on the back. Writing later.

                                                                    Howard

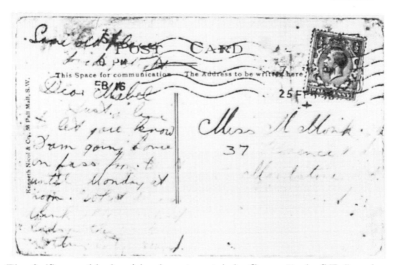

Fig. 9. 'Same old place' is almost certainly Grove Park, S.E. London.

Fig. 10. (Reverse of Fig. 9.) Probably taken at the end of training. A class was usually eight trainees.

93

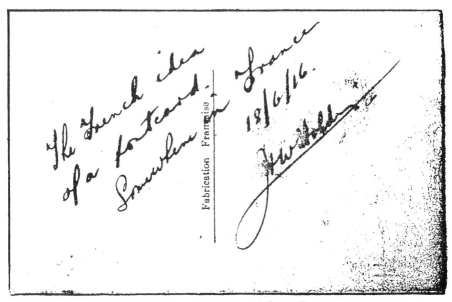

Fig. 11. The first postcard from France.

Fig. 12. Taken after the war.

Besides the medal with the regimental number, Figs. 9–12 show all that was available in hard evidence to trace the author's father.

ABBREVIATIONS USED IN THE TEXT

It will soon be obvious to the researcher that abbreviations are not the invention of the second half of the 20th Century. A glance at Fig. 8 will prove the point. During the course of the research, most abbreviations will become familiar, especially those applying to the branch of the Army concerned. However, the reader may find the list below a helpful start as most appear in the text. For uniformity, all initials appear without the interposed full stop. During the War no one style was universally used.

ADS	Advanced Dressing Station, a first aid post.
APS	Army Postal Service.
ASC	Army Service Corps. (Became RASC, Royal Army Service Corps, in 1919.)
AVS	Army Veterinary Service.
Bn., Bns.	Battalion(s). A unit of approximately 1,000 infantry.
BEF	British Expeditionary Force, the term used to describe the British Army in France.
Ref.	Refers to the Bibliography (page 47).
CCS	Casualty Clearing Station. An 800-bed tented hospital run by a Royal Army Medical Corps unit.
CO	Commanding Officer.
Coy., Cos.	Company, companies.
DDMS	Deputy Director of Medical Services.
Div.	Division. A unit of approximately 18,000 men.
Divnl.	Divisional. Attached to, or concerned with, a Division.
FA	Field Ambulance. An RAMC unit; not a vehicle.
GHQ	General Headquarters. Used for both the location and organisation.
HQ	Headquarters. Used for both the location and organisation.
i/c	as in 'Officer i/c'. The Officer in Command of the unit in question.
IWM	Imperial War Museum, London.
L of C	Lines of Communication.
MAC	Motor Ambulance Convoy. An RAMC unit.
MGC	Machine Gun Corps.
NCO	Non-Commissioned Officer, e.g. Sergeant or Corporal.
Note	Refers to the list of Notes (page 54).
PRO	Public Record Office, Kew.
RA	Royal Artillery. (Colloquially, The Gunners.)
RAMC	Royal Army Medical Corps.
RAOC	Royal Army Ordnance Corps.
RE	Royal Engineers. (Colloquially, The Sappers.)
RN	Royal Navy.